History K
Student Guide

Part 1

About K12 Inc.

K12 Inc. (NYSE: LRN) drives innovation and advances the quality of education by delivering state-of-the-art digital learning platforms and technology to students and school districts around the world. K12 is a company of educators offering its online and blended curriculum to charter schools, public school districts, private schools, and directly to families. More information can be found at K12.com.

978-1-60153-368-5

Printed by LSC Communications, Harrisonburg, VA, USA, May 2019.

Table of Contents

Unit 8: North America: From Maple Leaf to Cactus Branch

Unit 9: America the Beautiful

Unit 10: The First Americans

Answer Keys

Student Guide
Lesson 1: Our Earth, Our Home

Lesson Objectives

- Explore concepts to be addressed during the year in History K.
- State that Earth is the name of our world.
- Recognize the globe as a model of Earth.
- State that there are seven continents.

PREPARE

Approximate lesson time is 45 minutes.

Advance Preparation

- It's important that you read the Course Introduction for History K before your student begins the course. You can find the course introduction at the beginning of the Our Earth, Our Home lesson.
- It's important that you read the course introduction for Kindergarten History before you begin the first lesson. You can find it in the Help section of the Online School.

Materials

For the Student

    globe, inflatable

    ⌨ Continent Echo Song sheet

    ⌨ Continent Sights activity sheet

    folder, manila

    crayons, 16 or more

    scissors, round-end safety

Optional

    Floating Home by David Getz

    Where Do I Live? by Neil Chesanow

Keywords and Pronunciation

continent : One of the seven large pieces of land on Earth.

Earth : The planet on which we live; our world.

globe : A model of Earth.

North Pole : the northern tip of Earth

South Pole : The southern tip of Earth.

LEARN
Activity 1: Welcome to History K *(Online)*

Activity 2: Where in the World? *(Online)*

Activity 3: Blast Off! *(Online)*

Activity 4: Back on Earth *(Online)*

Activity 5: Sing a Song of Continents *(Online)*

Activity 6: Find the Continent *(Online)*

Activity 7: Color the Continents *(Online)*

ASSESS
Lesson Assessment: Our Earth, Our Home (*Online*)
You will complete an offline assessment covering the main objectives of this lesson. Your learning coach will score this assessment.

LEARN
Activity 8. Optional: Our Great Big World *(Online)*

Continent Echo Song

Adult: North America
Child: North America
Adult: South America
Child: South America
Adult: Antarctica
Child: Antarctica
Adult: And Africa
Child: And Africa
Together: North America
Together: South America
Together: Antarctica
Together: And Africa

Adult: Europe, Asia
Child: Europe, Asia
Adult: And Australia
Child: And Australia
Adult: South Pole, North Pole
Child: South Pole, North Pole
Adult: And that's my world
Child: And that's my world
Together: Europe, Asia
Together: And Australia
Together: South Pole, North Pole
Together: And that's my world

cut

Lesson Assessment

Our Home, Our Earth

1. What is the name of our world?

2. What is the globe a model of?

3. How many continents are there?

Student Guide
Lesson 2: Name That Continent

Lesson Objectives

- Begin to recognize the names of the seven continents.
- Recognize a map of the world as a flat model of the globe.

PREPARE

Approximate lesson time is 45 minutes.

Materials

For the Student

  globe, inflatable

  map, world

  tape, masking

  plants, small green

  soil, potting

  jar, large glass

  ⏚ Continent Echo Song sheet, version 2

Optional

  ⏚ map of the world

  ⏚ Map of the World Puzzle Pieces

  scissors, round-end safety

  coin

Keywords and Pronunciation

world map : A flat picture of the world.

LEARN
Activity 1: Sing and Find *(Online)*

Activity 2: The Continents: Which Is Which? *(Online)*

Activity 3: Continent Echo Song *(Online)*

Activity 4: Globe Toss (Online)

Activity 5. Optional: Map Matching (Online)

ASSESS

Lesson Assessment: Name That Continent (*Online*)

You will complete an offline assessment covering the main objectives of this lesson. Your learning coach will score this assessment.

LEARN

Activity 6. Optional: Coin Toss (Online)

Continent Echo Song
Version 2

Child: North America
Adult: A canyon grand
Child: South America
Adult: Rainforest land
Child: Antarctica
Adult: The snow is high
Child: And Africa
Adult: The desert's dry
Together: North America
Together: South America
Together: Antarctica
Together: And Africa

Child: Europe, Asia
Adult: Castles, great wall
Child: And Australia
Adult: Best reef of all
Child: South Pole, North Pole
Adult: Bottom and top
Child: And that's my world
Adult: It's time to stop
Together: Europe, Asia
Together: And Australia
Together: South Pole, North Pole
Together: And that's my world

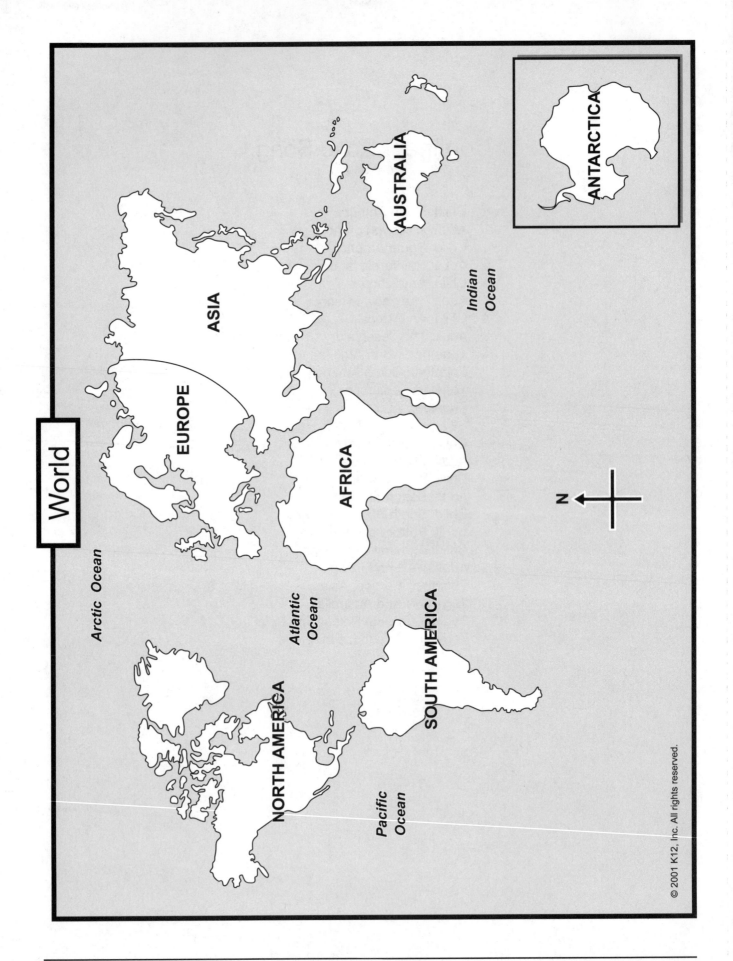

World

ARCTIC Ocean

ASIA

EUROPE

AFRICA

AUSTRALIA

Indian Ocean

ANTARCTICA

N

Atlantic Ocean

NORTH AMERICA

SOUTH AMERICA

Pacific Ocean

World Map Puzzle Pieces

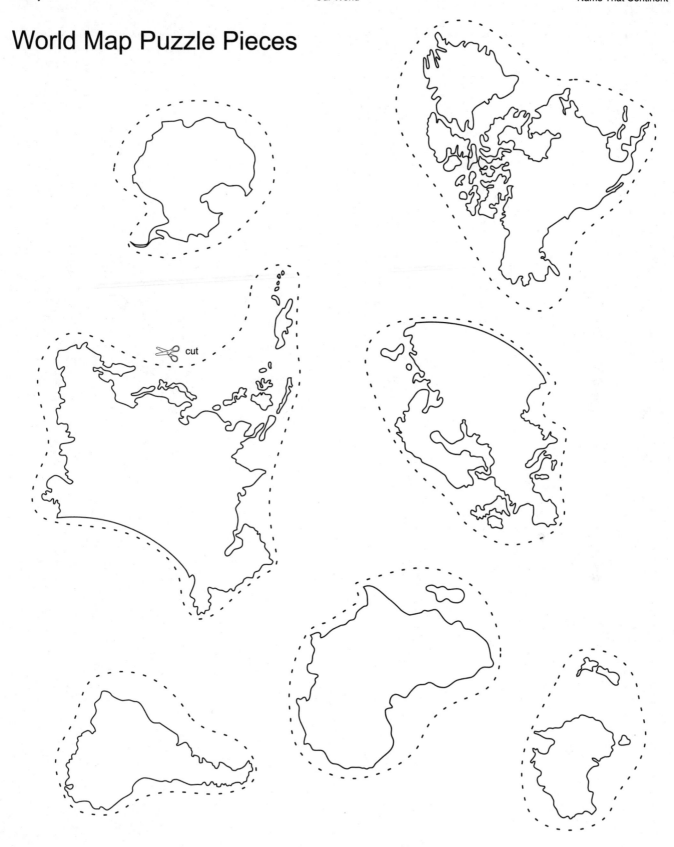

cut

Name _____ Date _____

Lesson Assessment

Name That Continent

1. What is a flat model of the globe called?

2. During Globe toss, can you identify each continent and the sight associated with it?

Student Guide
Lesson 3: Moving in the Right Direction

Lesson Objectives
- Locate the North and South Poles on a globe.
- Recognize the four cardinal directions: north, south, east, and west.

PREPARE

Approximate lesson time is 45 minutes.

Materials

For the Student

> globe, inflatable
>
> Mr. Traveler Figurine
>
> map, world

Optional

> 🖳 Compass Rose activity sheet
>
> 🖳 Compass Rose Comparison sheet
>
> crayons, 16 or more
>
> compass

Keywords and Pronunciation

compass rose : A symbol on maps and globes to point the way north, south, east, and west.

east : One of the four main points of the compass. The sun rises in the east.

north : One of the four main points of the compass.

south : One of the four main points of the compass.

west : One of the four main points of the compass. The sun sets in the west.

LEARN
Activity 1: Traveling Around the World (Online)

Activity 2: Discovering North, South, East, and West (Online)

Activity 3: Moving on a Map (Online)

Activity 4. Optional: North, East, South, and West (Online)

ASSESS

Lesson Assessment: Moving in the Right Direction (Online)

You will complete an offline assessment covering the main objectives of this lesson. Your learning coach will score this assessment.

LEARN

Activity 5. Optional: Sun Up, Sun Down (Online)

Activity 6. Optional: Using a Compass (Online)

Name _____   Date _____

Compass Rose

Write the letters *S, E,* and *W* near the corresponding points of the compass rose to indicate the directions south, east, and west.

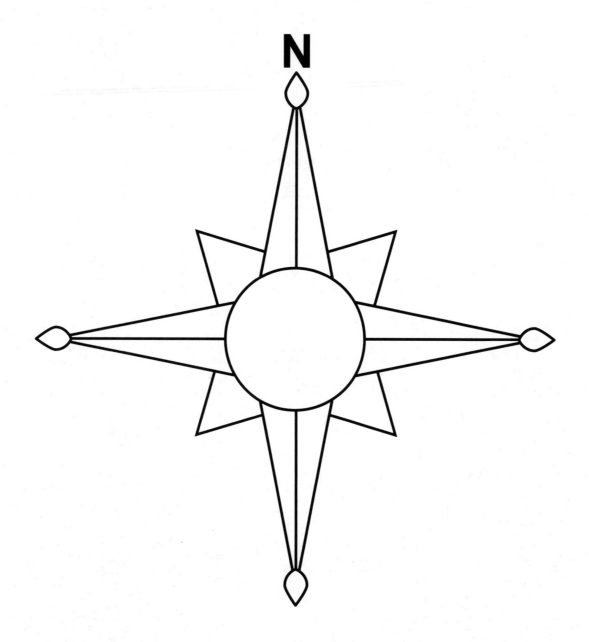

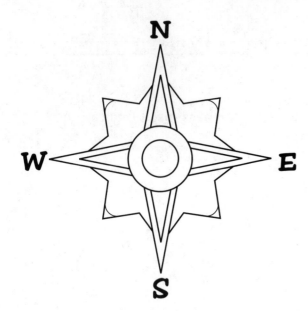

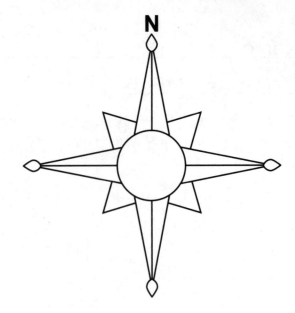

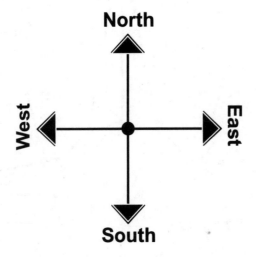

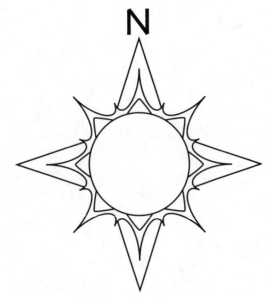

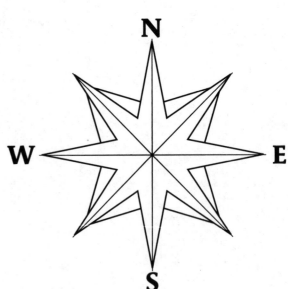

Lesson Assessment

Moving in the Right Direction

Use Mr. Traveler and the world map to complete the questions.

1. Put Mr. Traveler on the world map and move him north, south, east, and west.

2. Place Mr. Traveler on the world map and walk him to the North and South Poles.

Student Guide
Lesson 4: Get Ready to Travel

Lesson Objectives

- Locate own continent and country on the globe.
- Name own continent.
- Name own country.

PREPARE

Approximate lesson time is 45 minutes.

Materials

For the Student

 globe, inflatable

 Mr. Traveler Figurine

 🖳 map of the world

 stickers, small round red

 crayons, 16 or more

 tape, masking

 🖳 Passport Information sheet

 pencils, no. 2

 photo, personal

 scales

 Elmer's Glue-All

 measuring tape

 map, world

Optional

 🖳 Suitcase Cover sheet

 folder, manila

 stickers

 tape, clear

 As the Crow Flies: A First Book of Maps by Gail Hartman

 Me on the Map by Joan Sweeney

Keywords and Pronunciation

passport : An official paper that gives you permission to travel to another country.

LEARN
Activity 1: Getting Ready to Go! *(Online)*

Activity 2: Continent and Country *(Online)*

Activity 3: Make Your Own Passport *(Online)*

Activity 4: My Country, My Continent *(Online)*

Activity 5. Optional: Packing a Suitcase *(Online)*

ASSESS
Lesson Assessment: Get Ready to Travel (*Online*)
You will complete an offline assessment covering the main objectives of this lesson. Your learning coach will score this assessment.

LEARN
Activity 6. Optional: Read All About It! *(Online)*

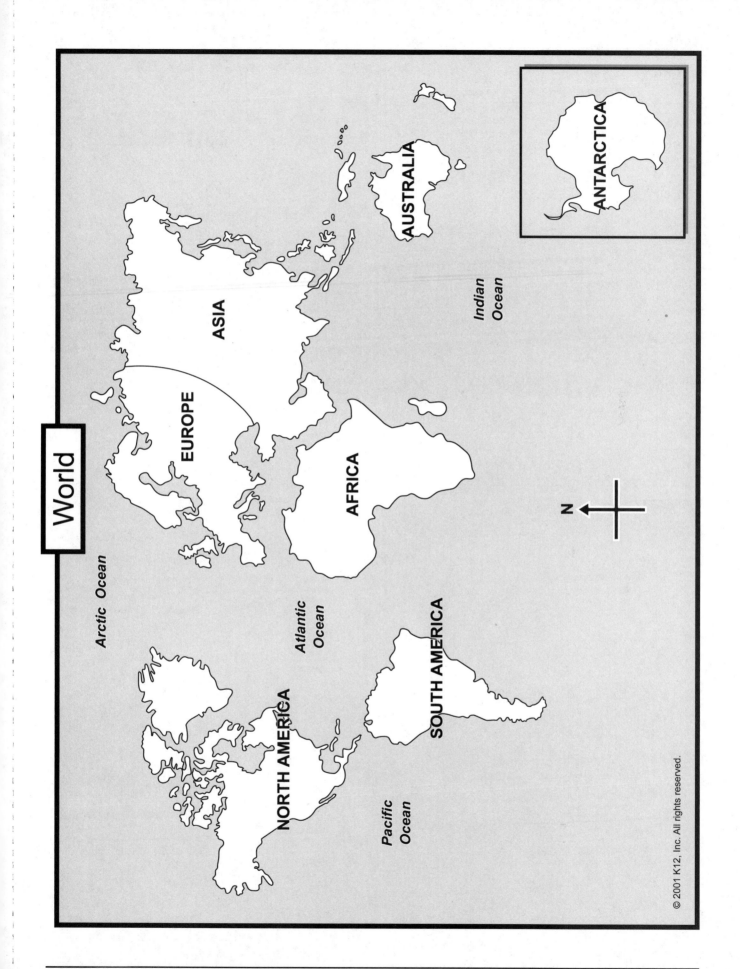

World

ANTARCTICA

ASIA

AUSTRALIA

Indian Ocean

EUROPE

AFRICA

Arctic Ocean

N

NORTH AMERICA

Atlantic Ocean

SOUTH AMERICA

Pacific Ocean

PASSPORT INFORMATION

COMPLETE NAME _____

CONTINENT _____

COUNTRY _____

STREET ADDRESS _____

TOWN OR CITY _____

STATE _____

ZIP CODE _____

PHONE NUMBER _____

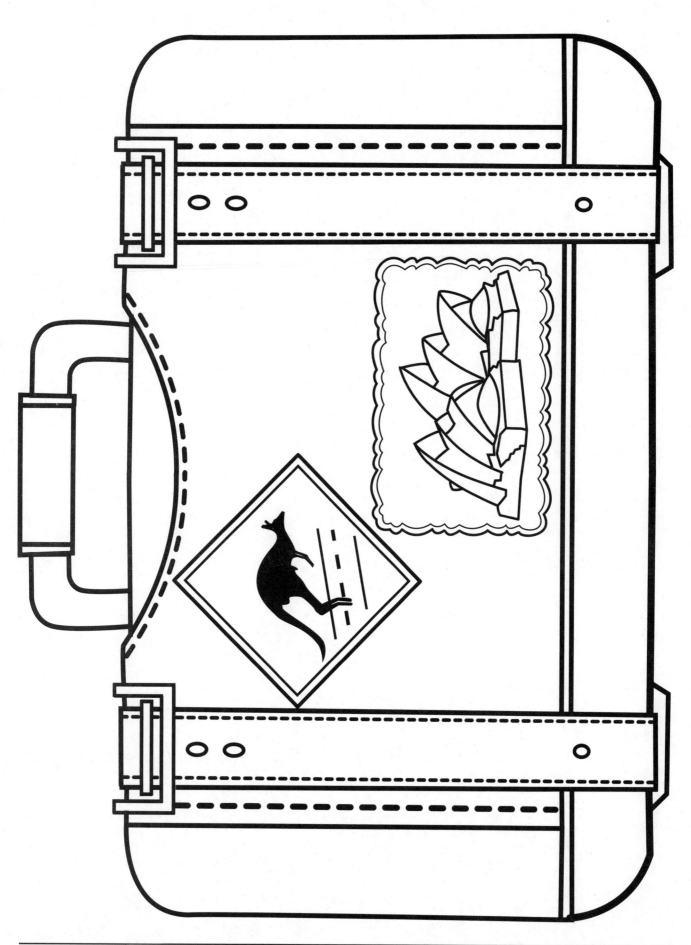

Lesson Assessment

Get Ready to Travel

1. Which continent do you live on?

2. Which country do you live in?

3. Place the Mr. Traveler on the globe and move him in a circle around the continent on which you live and around the country in which you live.

Student Guide
Lesson 1: Animals of the Outback

Lesson Objectives
- Identify three animals that are native to Australia.
- Know that Australia is a continent.
- Locate Australia on a world map.

PREPARE

Approximate lesson time is 45 minutes.

Materials

For the Student

    globe, inflatable

    map, world

    Possum Magic by Mem Fox (ISBN 152632247.000)

    📖 map of Australia

    Mr. Traveler Figurine

    📖 The Kookaburra Song

    📖 Animals of Australia activity sheet

    crayons, 16 or more

    Elmer's Glue-All

    index cards, 4" x 6" (6)

    scissors, round-end safety

Optional

    Koala Lou by Mem Fox

    One Wooly Wombat by Rod Trinca

    Snap by Marcia Vaughan

    Wombat Goes Walkabout by Michael Morpurgo

Keywords and Pronunciation

coast : The land along the edge of a body of water.

echidna (ih-KID-nuh)

emu (EE-myoo)

eucalyptus (yoo-kuh-LIP-tuhs)

kookaburra (KOO-kuh-bur-uh)

platypus (PLA-tih-puhs)

LEARN
Activity 1: Introduction to Australia *(Online)*

Activity 2: Possum Magic *(Online)*

Activity 3: Getting to Know Australia's Geography *(Online)*

Activity 4: Unusual Animals *(Online)*

Activity 5: Sing a Kookaburra Song *(Online)*

Activity 6: Animal Friends from Australia *(Online)*

ASSESS
Lesson Assessment: Animals of the Outback (*Online*)
You will complete an offline assessment covering the main objectives of this lesson. Your learning coach will score this assessment.

LEARN
Activity 7. Optional: Books to Read *(Online)*

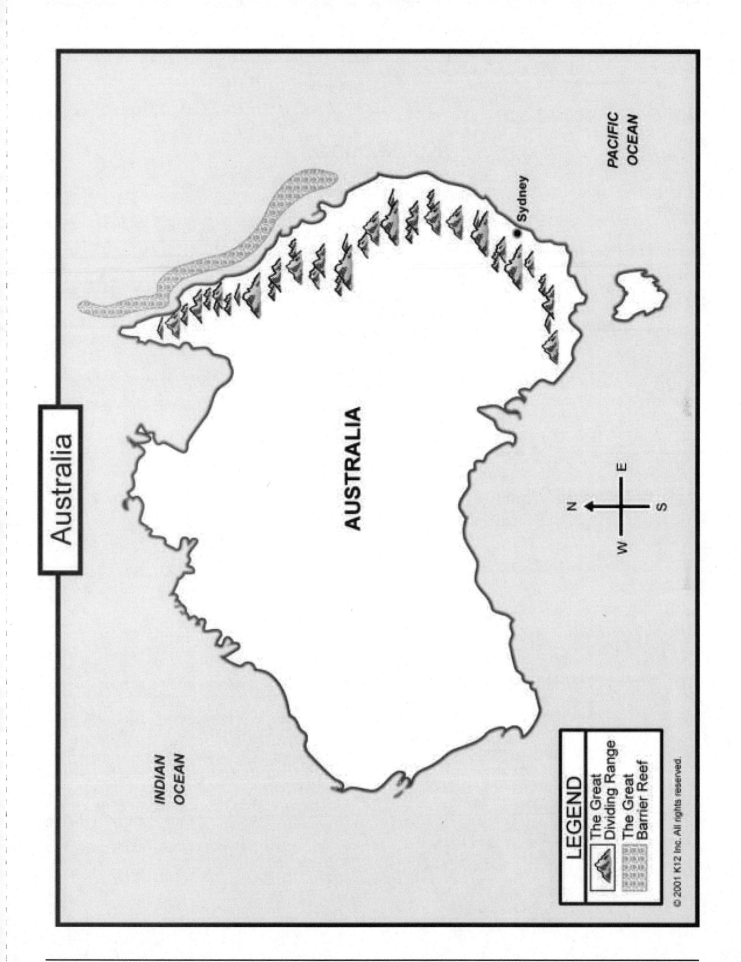

Australia

PACIFIC OCEAN

INDIAN OCEAN

AUSTRALIA

Sydney

N E S W

LEGEND
The Great Dividing Range
The Great Barrier Reef

© 2001 K12 Inc. All rights reserved.

Kookaburra

Kookaburra sits in the old gum tree,
Merry, merry king of the bush is he.
Laugh, Kookaburra, laugh, Kookaburra,
Gay your life must be.

Kookaburra sits in the old gum tree,
Eating all the gumdrops he can see.
Stop, Kookaburra, stop, Kookaburra,
Save some gums for me.

Kookaburra sits in the old gum tree,
Counting all the monkeys he can see.
Stop, Kookaburra, stop, Kookaburra,
That's no monkey, that's me!

Animals of Australia

Color in all the Australian animals. Name the animals you have colored. Cut out only the Australian animals and glue them to index cards. Place the cards in your Australia suitcase.

cut

Lesson Assessment

Animals of the Outback

Use the world map to complete the first question.

1. Locate Australia on the world map.

2. Name three well-known Australian animals that you colored.

3. What is Australia?

Student Guide
Lesson 2: Outback and City

Lesson Objectives

- Locate the coastline on a map of Australia.
- Recognize Sydney as a coastal city of Australia.

PREPARE

Approximate lesson time is 45 minutes.

Materials

For the Student

> globe, inflatable
>
> 🖳 map of Australia

Optional

> crayons, 16 or more
>
> index cards, 4" x 6" (2)
>
> cans, tin (2)
>
> string - nylon, about 20 feet

Keywords and Pronunciation

billabong (BIH-luh-bawng)

equator : An imaginary line around the middle of the Earth.

port city : A city built on a body of water where large ships can load and unload cargo.

LEARN
Activity 1: Checking Out the Globe *(Online)*

Activity 2: Jessica the Jillaroo *(Online)*

Activity 3: Sydney , the Coastal City *(Online)*

Activity 4. Optional: Postcards from Australia *(Online)*

ASSESS
Lesson Assessment: Outback and City (*Online*)
You will complete an offline assessment covering the main objectives of this lesson. Your learning coach will score this assessment.

LEARN
Activity 5. Optional: School of the Air (*Online*)

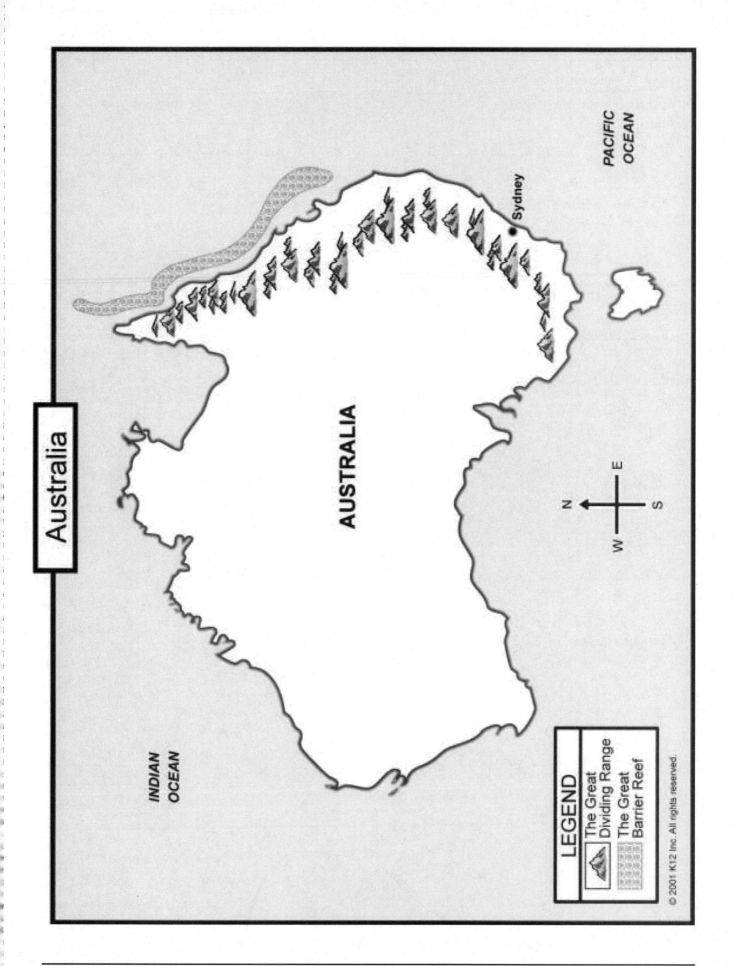

Australia

AUSTRALIA

Sydney

PACIFIC
OCEAN

INDIAN
OCEAN

N
W — E
S

LEGEND
The Great
Dividing Range
The Great
Barrier Reef

© 2001 K12 Inc. All rights reserved.

Lesson Assessment

Outback and City

Use the map of Australia to complete the first question.

1. Point to the coastline of Australia.

2. Is Sydney a coastal city?

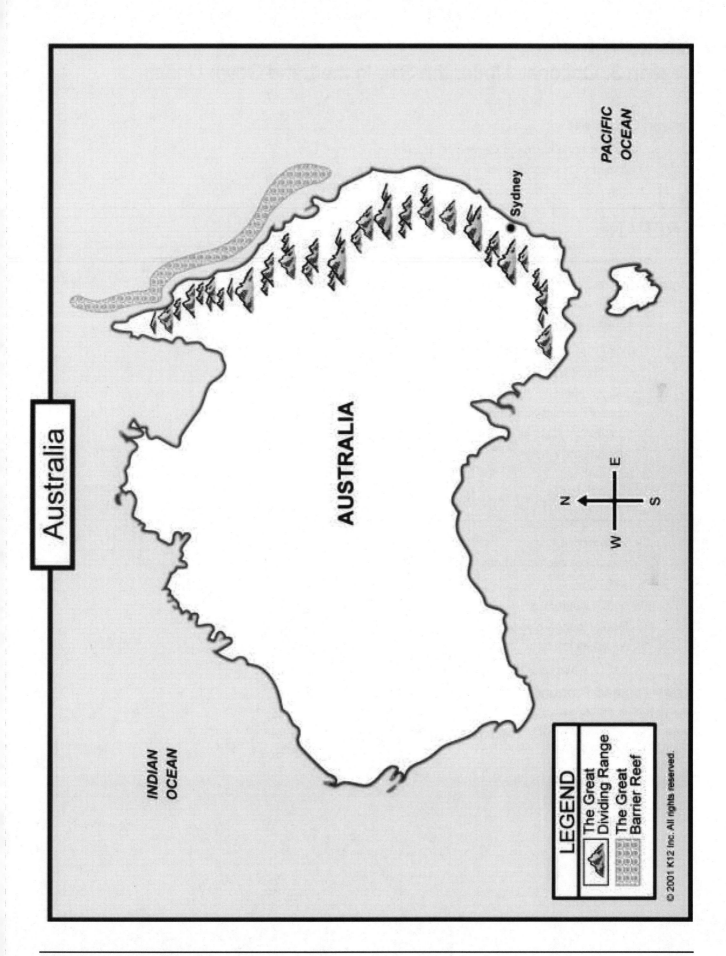

Australia

AUSTRALIA

INDIAN
OCEAN

PACIFIC
OCEAN

Sydney

N
W — E
S

LEGEND

The Great
Dividing Range

The Great
Barrier Reef

© 2001 K12 Inc. All rights reserved.

Student Guide
Lesson 3. Optional: Under the Sea in the Land Down Under

Lesson Objectives

- Identify marine life in the Great Barrier Reef.
- Locate the Great Barrier Reef on a map of Australia.

PREPARE

Approximate lesson time is 45 minutes.

Materials

For the Student

- 🖥 map of Australia
- 🖥 Barrier Reef playing cards
- 🖥 Definitions sheet
- paper, heavy
- scissors, round-end safety
- 🖥 Coral Wall sheet
- crayons, 16 or more
- Elmer's Glue-All
- plastic wrap - blue
- shoeboxes
- tape, clear
- paper, colored construction, 12"x12" - white
- salt (12)
- brush, watercolor
- food coloring - blue, yellow, red, green
- jar, small (7)
- paints, watercolor, 8 colors or more

Keywords and Pronunciation

anemone (uh-NEH-muh-nee)

coral : The hard remains of a type of sea creature that gather to form a reef.

dugong (DOO-gawng)

reef : A wall of rocks or coral that is built up to the surface of a body of water.

LEARN

Activity 1. Optional: Optional Lesson Instructions *(Online)*

This lesson is OPTIONAL. It is provided for students who seek enrichment or extra practice. You may skip this lesson.

If you choose to skip this lesson, then go to the Plan or Lesson Lists page and mark this lesson "Skipped" in order to proceed to the next lesson in the course.

Activity 2. Optional: Sing and Find *(Online)*

Activity 3. Optional: Marine Life in the Great Barrier Reef *(Online)*

Activity 4. Optional: Marine Life *(Online)*

Activity 5. Optional: Great Barrier Reef Fish *(Online)*

Activity 6. Optional: Make a Coral Reef Diorama *(Online)*

Activity 7. Optional: Saltwater Picture *(Online)*

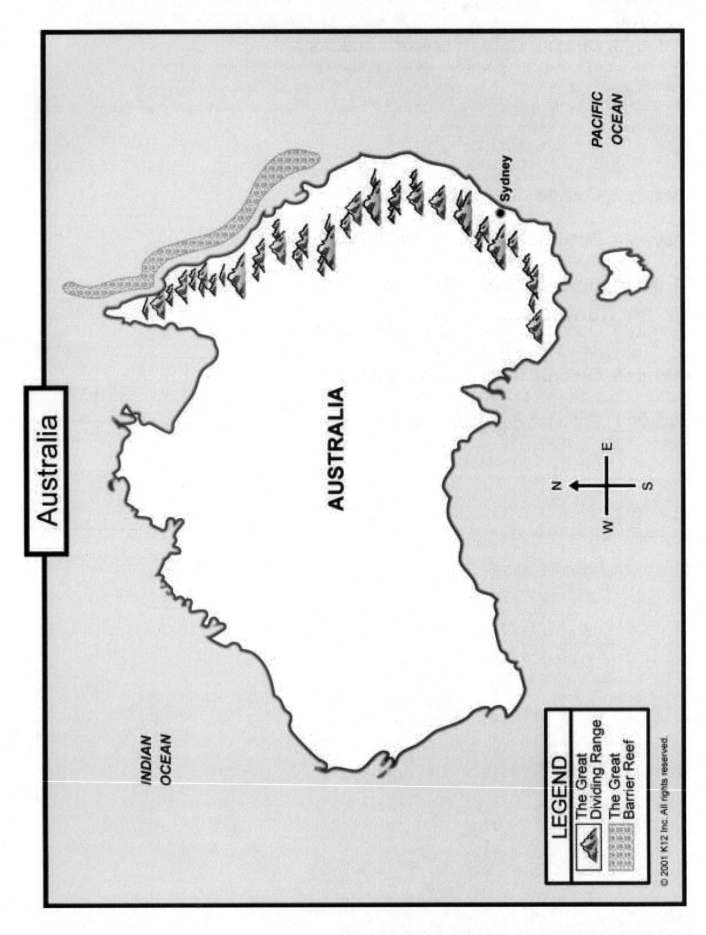

Australia

PACIFIC OCEAN

Sydney

AUSTRALIA

INDIAN OCEAN

N
W E
S

LEGEND

The Great Dividing Range

The Great Barrier Reef

© 2001 K12 Inc. All rights reserved.

cut

Dugong

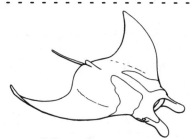

Manta ray

Humpback whale

Mud crab

Giant clam

Sea snake

Sea anemone

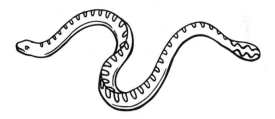

Crown-of-thorns starfish

Green turtle

Bottle-nosed dolphin

The **GIANT CLAM** has a soft body protected by two hard shells. It has a zigzag mouth that's as long as your front door is wide. The giant clam lives in the sand and the mud at the bottom of the sea—and sucks in food that swims by.

The **GREEN TURTLE** is one of the largest turtles in the world. The green turtle grows as big as a car tire and weighs more than most adult humans. Laws have been written to protect these creatures because there aren't many of them left.

The **MUD CRAB** is a flat sea creature with four pairs of legs (that's a total of eight), two pincers, and short antennae. Mud crabs move sideways instead of forward, and if one of their two pincers falls off, another will grow back.

The **DUGONG** is sometimes called a sea cow. Sea cows chew on sea grass with their long teeth. They do not move very fast and have to come up for air every 10 to 15 minutes.

The **SEA SNAKE** is one of the most poisonous creatures on the reef, but it is also very shy. Sea snakes usually hide in the coral reef when they see a human. They have a special flat tail that helps them swim through the water.

The **MANTA RAY** is a flat, square-shaped sea creature with a long tail and fins like wings. The manta ray likes to hide under the sand of the ocean floor.

The **SEA ANEMONE** is a brightly colored animal that looks like a flower. The sea anemone uses its petal-like arms to catch food and scoop it into its mouth. Sea anemones have been known to sting anyone who tries to remove them from the coral reef.

The **CROWN-OF-THORNS STARFISH** has 16 to 18 arms covered with spines. It can move easily in any direction using its suction-cup feet. A hungry crown-of-thorns starfish likes to eat coral, which damages the reef.

The **HUMPBACK WHALE** is a very acrobatic sea creature. It's called a humpback because of the big fin on its back and because it arches its back way up when it gets ready to dive beneath the water.

The **BOTTLE-NOSED DOLPHIN** has a thick body and a snout that sticks out like a beak. These dolphins are friendly and like to swim with humans as well as whales.

Where are these animals usually found?

Giant clam—on the ocean floor
Green turtle—on the ocean floor
Mud crab—on the ocean floor
Sea snake—hiding in the coral reef or swimming in the ocean
Manta ray—on the ocean floor, sometimes hiding under the sand
Sea anemone—on the wall of the coral reef
Crown-of-thorns starfish—on the wall of the coral reef
Dugong—near the sea grass on the ocean floor or swimming up for air
Bottle-nosed dolphin—swimming in the ocean, sometimes near the surface
Humpback whale—swimming in the ocean, sometimes near the surface

---

Student Guide
Lesson 1: Let's Visit Spain

Lesson Objectives

- Know that Spain is in Europe.
- Locate Europe on a globe.
- Recognize a country as part of a continent.

PREPARE

Approximate lesson time is 45 minutes.

Materials

For the Student

- 🖳 Suitcase activity sheet
- folder, manila
- globe, inflatable
- crayons, 16 or more
- Elmer's Glue-All
- map, world
- stapler
- 🖳 map of Europe
- 🖳 national flag of Spain
- Mr. Traveler Figurine
- 🖳 Hide and Seek in Spain activity sheet
- pencils, no. 2
- The Story of Ferdinand by Munro Leaf (ISBN 0140502343)

Optional

- paper, drawing
- The Beautiful Butterfly: A Folktale from Spain by Judy Sierra

Keywords and Pronunciation

country : An area that is usually smaller than a continent, where the people have the same flag, money, and laws.

Madrid (muh-DRID)

matador (MA-tuh-dawr)

LEARN
Activity 1: Preparing to Travel *(Online)*

Activity 2: Exploring Spain *(Online)*

Activity 3: Hide and Seek in Spain *(Online)*

Activity 4: A Story About a Bull *(Online)*

Activity 5. Optional: Making Choices *(Online)*

ASSESS
Lesson Assessment: Let's Visit Spain (*Online*)

You will complete an offline assessment covering the main objectives of this lesson. Your learning coach will score this assessment.

LEARN
Activity 6. Optional: Reading a Spanish Folktale *(Online)*

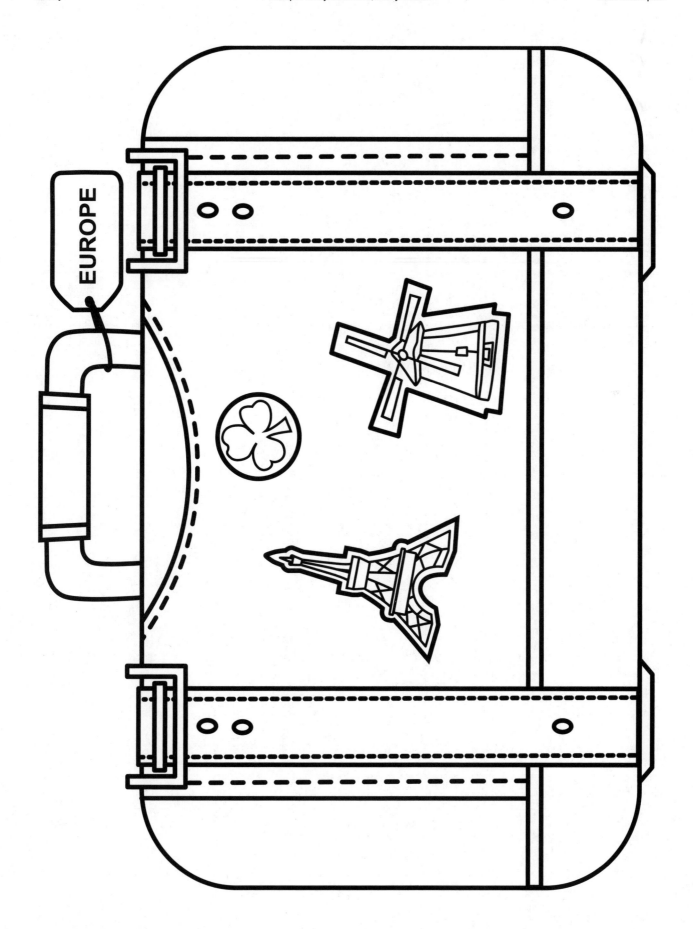

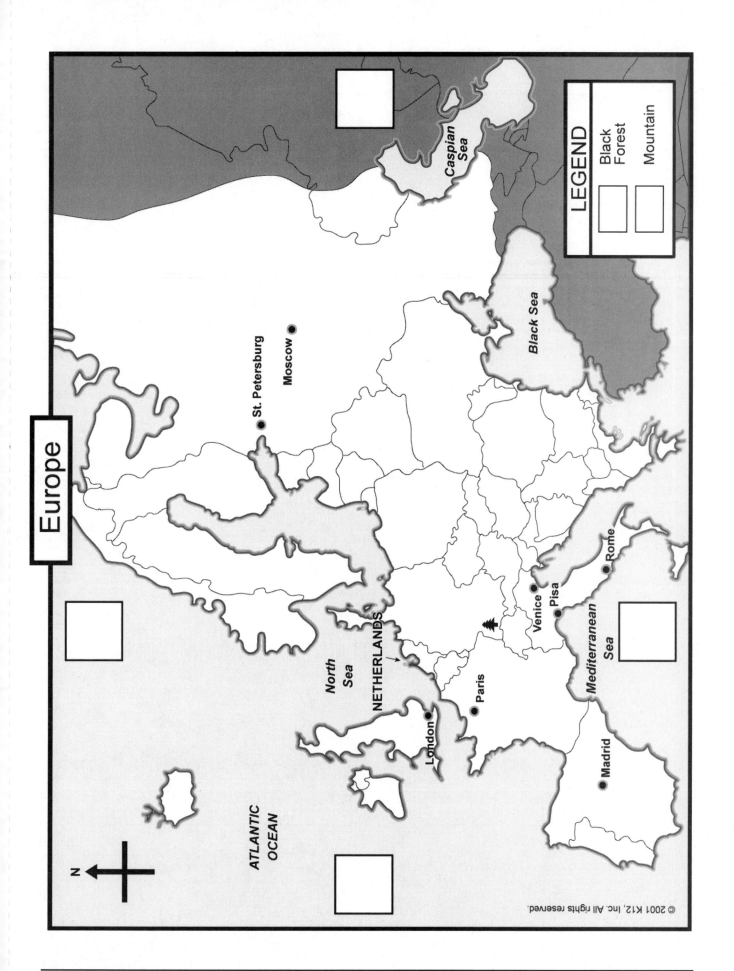

Europe

LEGEND

Black Forest

Mountain

Caspian Sea

Black Sea

St. Petersburg

Moscow

Rome

Venice

Pisa

Mediterranean Sea

North Sea

NETHERLANDS

Paris

London

Madrid

ATLANTIC OCEAN

N

61

Red

Yellow

Red

Spain

Hide and Seek in Spain

Listen carefully to the story while it is read out loud. When you see a picture of something named in the story, draw a circle around it.

Once there was a **king** who lived in a city in Spain called Madrid. He often sat and looked down at his kingdom from a tall tower in his **castle.**

There were lots of castles in Spain. For many years, armies from neighboring kingdoms had attacked the king's city. They would throw spears and shoot flaming arrows over the top of the **stone wall** that protected the city. But the stone wall that protected the city was so high and so thick that the armies could not get inside to hurt the people of Madrid.

Now when the King of Madrid looked out over the walls, he saw neat **rows of grain,** green and tall, reaching toward the sky. In a few months, the grain would ripen and turn golden-brown. Then the farmers would cut down the grain to be made into bread to feed all the people living in Madrid.

The king also saw acres upon acres of **grapevines** and **cork trees.**
Cattle roamed the hills in search of grass, and children herded them along to make sure none were lost.

When night began to fall, all the children, farmers, and cattle would come back through the city gate and return to their homes inside the city wall. The King of Madrid smiled to himself. His city was one of the best in Spain, because of the strong stone wall that protected his people.

Lesson Assessment

Let's Visit Spain

Use the globe to complete the first question.

1. Locate Europe on the globe.

2. What is a country a part of?

3. What continent is Spain located on?

Student Guide
Lesson 2: Let's Visit England

Lesson Objectives

- Know that an island is a piece of land surrounded by water.
- Locate Europe on a globe.
- Recognize that England is in Europe.

PREPARE

Approximate lesson time is 45 minutes.

Materials

For the Student

    map, world

    ⌨ map of Europe

    Mr. Traveler Figurine

    crayons, 16 or more

    ⌨ London Bridge Is Falling Down

Optional

    ⌨ British Flag coloring sheet

    ⌨ Double-Decker Bus activity sheet

    scissors, round-end safety

    Jack and the Beanstalk and Other Favorite Folktales illustrated by Richard Walz

    Tom Thumb illustrated by Richard Jesse Watson

Keywords and Pronunciation

island : A piece of land surrounded by water.

Thames (temz)

Trafalgar (truh-FAHL-gur)

LEARN
Activity 1: Geography Riddle Game *(Online)*

Activity 2: Traveling to England *(Online)*

Activity 3: Postcards from London *(Online)*

Activity 4: London's Bridge *(Online)*

Activity 5. Optional: Visiting the Sights *(Online)*

ASSESS
Lesson Assessment: Let's Visit England (*Online*)
You will complete an offline assessment covering the main objectives of this lesson. Your learning coach will score this assessment.

LEARN
Activity 6. Optional: Reading English Folktales *(Online)*

Activity 7. Optional: Fun Words to Learn *(Online)*

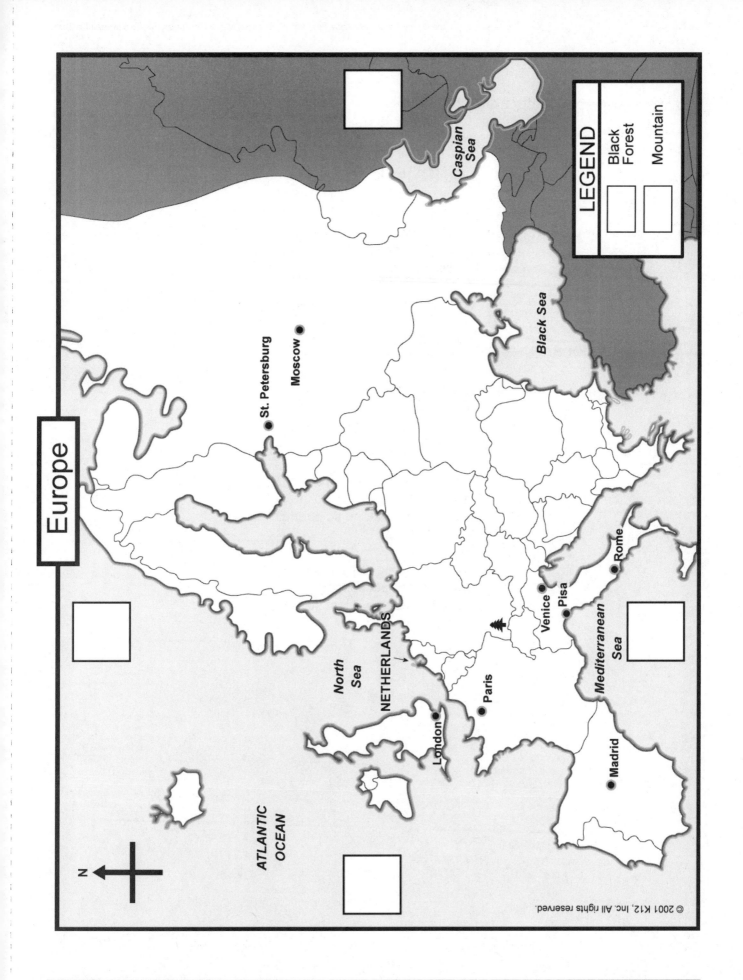

Europe

LEGEND

Black Forest

Mountain

Caspian Sea

Black Sea

Moscow

St. Petersburg

Rome

Pisa

Venice

Mediterranean Sea

North Sea

NETHERLANDS

Paris

London

Madrid

ATLANTIC OCEAN

N

London Bridge Is Falling Down

London Bridge is falling down,
Falling down, falling down.
London Bridge is falling down,
My fair lady.

Build it up with wood and clay,
Wood and clay, wood and clay.
Build it up with wood and clay,
My fair lady.

Wood and clay will wash away,
Wash away, wash away.
Wood and clay will wash away,
My fair lady.

Build it up with stone so strong,
Stone so strong, stone so strong.
Build it up with stone so strong,
My fair lady.

Stone so strong will last so long,
Last so long, last so long.
Stone so strong will last so long,
My fair lady.

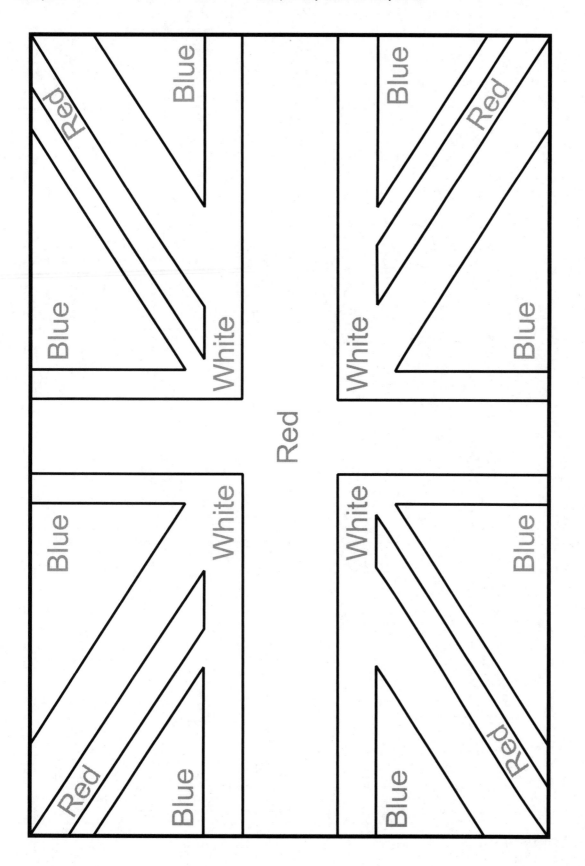

England is part of the United Kingdom

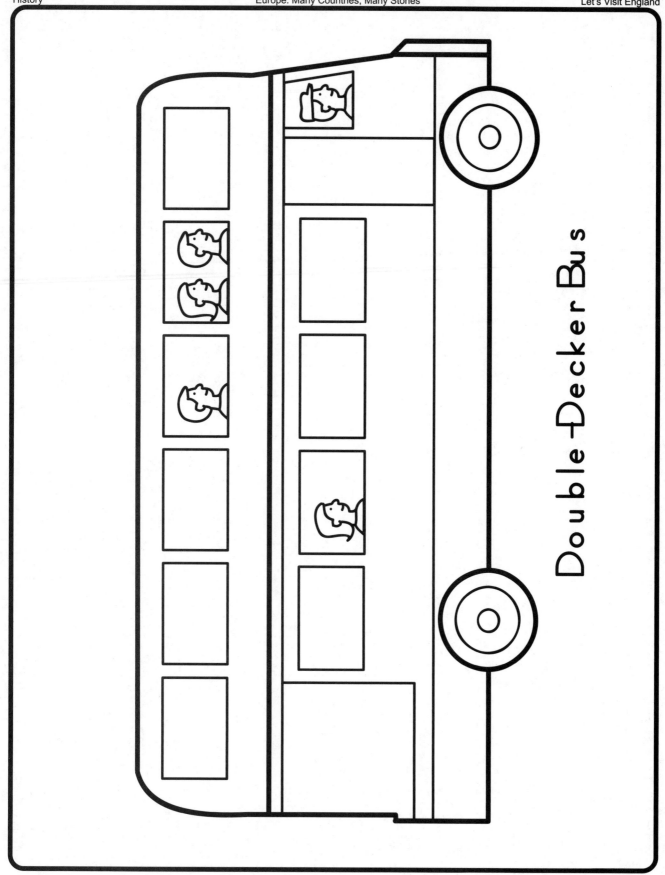

Double-Decker Bus

Lesson Assessment

Let's Visit England

Use the globe to complete the questions.

1. Locate Europe on the globe.

2. If you are in England, which continent are you on?

3. Locate an island on a globe or map and point to it while asking this question. Why do we say this piece of land is an island?

Student Guide
Lesson 3: Let's Visit France

Lesson Objectives

- Know that France is in Europe.
- Name two landmarks found in France.

PREPARE

Approximate lesson time is 45 minutes.

Materials

For the Student

   📖 map of Europe

   crayons, 16 or more

   Madeline by Ludwig Bemelmans (ISBN 0670445800)

   📖 Lyrics to Frere Jacques

Optional

   📖 French Flag coloring sheet

Keywords and Pronunciation

Clavel (klah-VEL)

Gustave Eiffel (GOUS-tahv IY-fuhl)

legend : A box found on a map that explains the meaning of certain signs and marks.

Louvre (loov)

Madeline (MA-duh-liyn)

mosaic (mo-ZAY-ik) : A decorative picture made by piecing together many colored tiles.

Notre Dame (noh-truh DAHM)

Sacré-Coeur (SAH-kray kour)

LEARN
Activity 1: Becoming Familiar with the Map (Online)

Activity 2: Reading About Madeline (Online)

Activity 3: Storybook Detective (Online)

Activity 4: Sing a French Song *(Online)*

Activity 5. Optional: The French Flag *(Online)*

ASSESS
Lesson Assessment: Let's Visit France (*Online*)
You will complete an offline assessment covering the main objectives of this lesson. Your learning coach will score this assessment.

LEARN
Activity 6. Optional: Visiting the Eiffel Tower *(Online)*

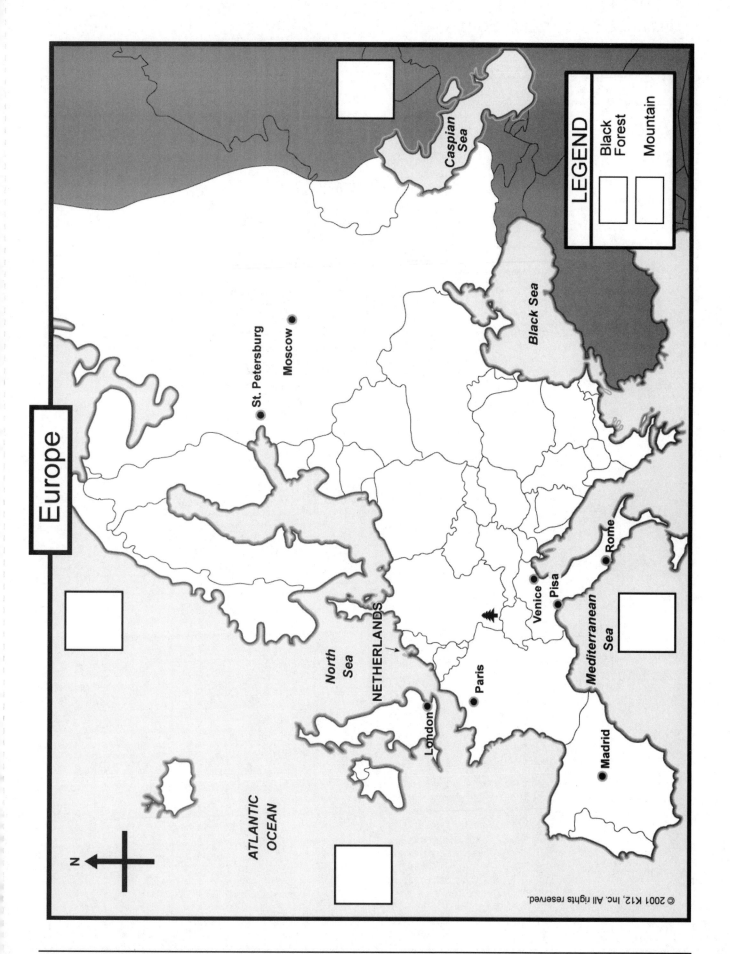

Europe

LEGEND
Black Forest
Mountain

Caspian Sea

Black Sea

St. Petersburg
Moscow

North Sea

NETHERLANDS

ATLANTIC OCEAN

London

Paris

Venice
Pisa
Rome

Mediterranean Sea

Madrid

N

Frére Jacques

Frére Jacques, Frére Jacques,
Dormez-vous? Dormez-vous?
Sonnez les matines,
Sonnez les matines,
Din, din, don! Din, din, don!

Are you sleeping? Are you sleeping?
Brother John? Brother John?
Morning bells are ringing,
Morning bells are ringing,
Ding, ding, dong. Ding, ding, dong.

Red

White

Blue

France

Lesson Assessment

Let's Visit France

1. Which continent is France on?

2. To answer this question, please remember what you've learned in the lesson and the book *Madeline*.
   What are the names of two landmarks found in France?

Student Guide
Lesson 4: Let's Visit Ireland

Lesson Objectives

- Associate Ireland with traditional figures and images, such as leprechauns and shamrocks.
- Explain why Ireland is called the Emerald Isle.
- Locate Ireland on a map of Europe.

PREPARE

Approximate lesson time is 45 minutes.

Materials

For the Student

    globe, inflatable

    🖳 map of Europe

    crayons, 16 or more

    🖳 Shamrock tracing sheet

    paper, colored construction, 12"x12"

    pen, ballpoint

    scissors, round-end safety

    tape, clear

Optional

    🖳 Flag of Ireland

    Jack and the Leprechaun by Ivan Robertson

    Jamie O'Rourke and the Big Potato by Tomie dePaola

    Leprechaun Gold by Teresa Bateman

    Tim O'Toole and the Wee Folk: An Irish Tale by Gerald McDermott

Keywords and Pronunciation

Finn McCool (fin mih-KOOL)

legend : An old story passed on by word of mouth.

leprechaun (LEP-ruh-kahn) : An elfish character in Irish legends who must reveal where his treasure is hidden if he is caught.

Una (OO-nah)

LEARN
Activity 1: Find the Continent *(Online)*

Activity 2: Geography Riddle Game *(Online)*

Activity 3: The Emerald Isle *(Online)*

Activity 4: Make a Shamrock *(Online)*

Activity 5: Leprechauns *(Online)*

Activity 6: The Giant Who Acted Like a Baby *(Online)*

Activity 7. Optional: The Flag of Ireland *(Online)*

ASSESS
Lesson Test: Let's Visit Ireland (*Online*)
You will complete an offline assessment covering the main objectives of this lesson. Your learning coach will score this assessment.

LEARN
Activity 8. Optional: Reading More Irish Legends *(Online)*

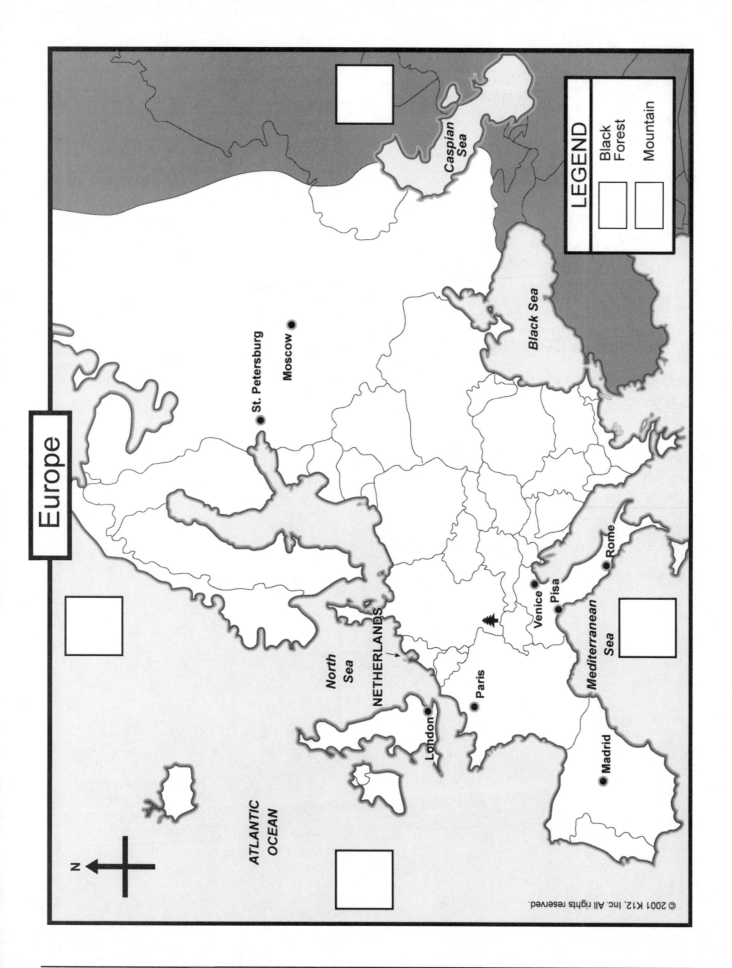

Europe

LEGEND

Black Forest

Mountain

Caspian Sea

Black Sea

St. Petersburg

Moscow

Rome

Venice

Pisa

Mediterranean Sea

North Sea

NETHERLANDS

Paris

London

Madrid

ATLANTIC OCEAN

N

Make a Shamrock

Orange

White

Green

Ireland

Lesson Assessment

Let's Visit Ireland

1. To answer this question, please use the attached map of Europe. Where is Ireland located?

2. What are two things you think about when you think of Ireland?

3. Why is Ireland nicknamed the Emerald Isle?

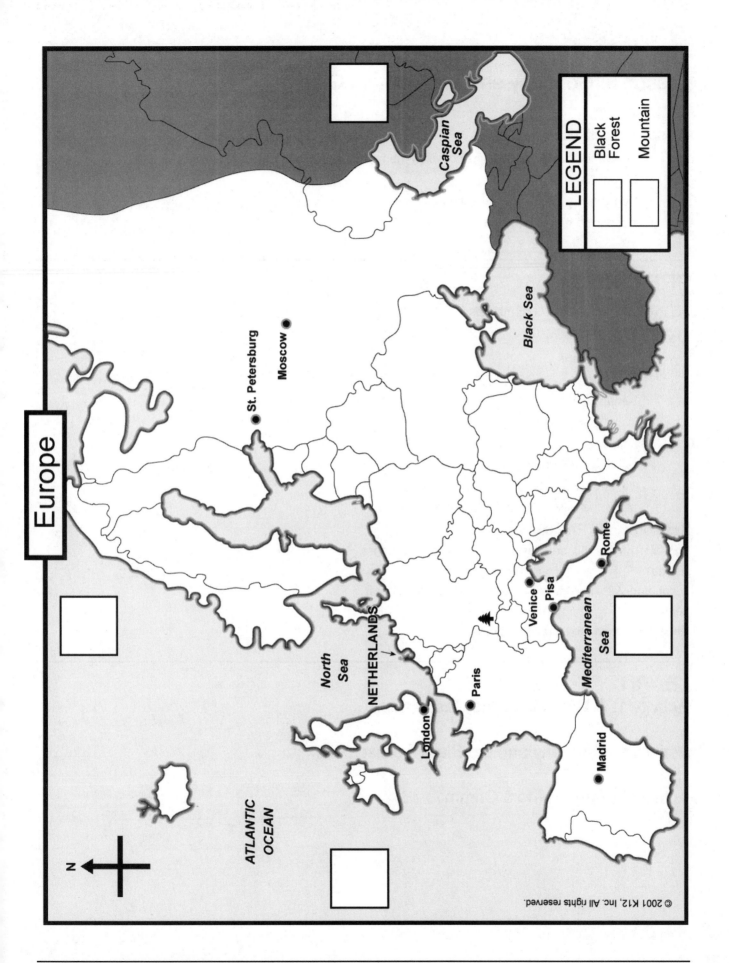

Europe

LEGEND

Black Forest

Mountain

Caspian Sea

Black Sea

St. Petersburg

Moscow

Rome

Venice

Pisa

Mediterranean Sea

North Sea

NETHERLANDS

Paris

London

Madrid

ATLANTIC OCEAN

N

Student Guide
Lesson 5: Germany and the Brothers Grimm

Lesson Objectives

- Know that the Grimm brothers collected many fairy tales, such as Snow White.
- Locate Europe on a globe.
- Recognize that countries are separated by borders.
- Recognize that Germany is in Europe.

PREPARE

Approximate lesson time is 45 minutes.

Materials

For the Student

- 🖳 map of Europe

    map, world

    crayons, 16 or more

Optional

- 🖳 Flag of Germany

    Rapunzel by Paul O. Zelinsky

    Rumpelstiltskin by Paul O. Zelinsky

Keywords and Pronunciation

border : The line that separates one country from another.

ja (yah)

Jacob and Wilhelm Grimm (YAH-kub and VIL-helm grim)

nein (niyn)

Neuschwanstein (noy-SHVAHN-stiyn)

LEARN
Activity 1: A World-Famous Castle (Online)

Activity 2: Germany and the Black Forest (Online)

Activity 3: The Brothers Grimm (Online)

Activity 4: Grimm's Fairy Tales *(Online)*

Activity 5: The Wolf and the Seven Little Kids *(Online)*

Activity 6. Optional: The German Flag *(Online)*

ASSESS

Lesson Assessment: Germany and the Brothers Grimm (*Online*)

You will complete an offline assessment covering the main objectives of this lesson. Your learning coach will score this assessment.

LEARN

Activity 7. Optional: Reading More Grimm's Fairy Tales *(Online)*

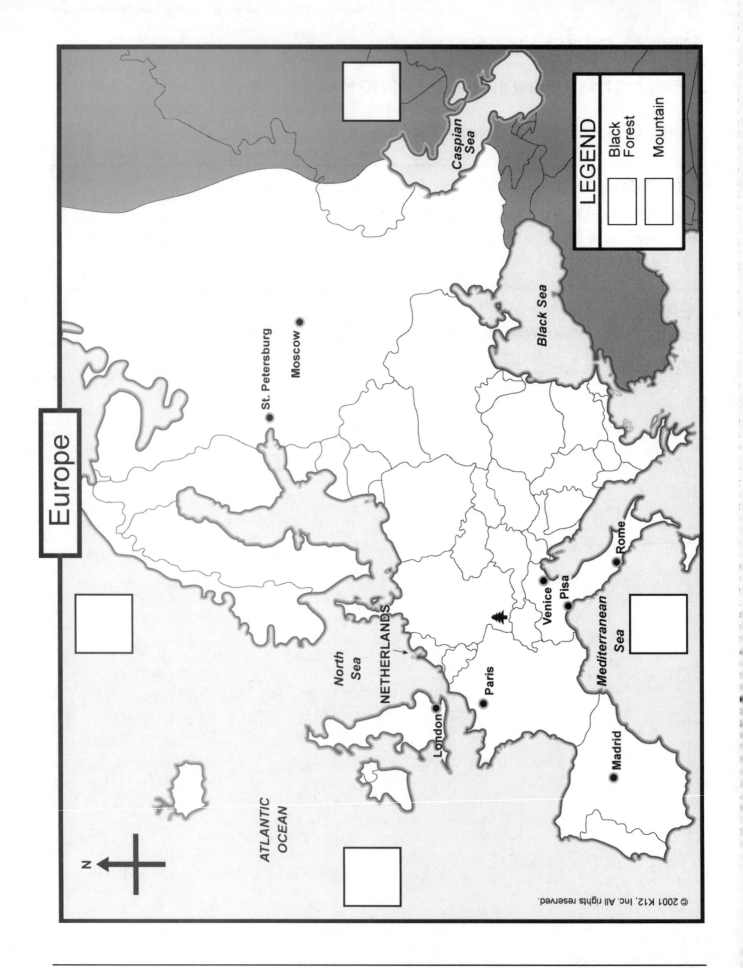

Europe

LEGEND

Black Forest

Mountain

Caspian Sea

Black Sea

St. Petersburg

Moscow

Mediterranean Sea

Venice
Pisa
Rome

North Sea

NETHERLANDS

Paris

London

ATLANTIC OCEAN

Madrid

N

Black	Red	Yellow

Germany

Name _____   Date _____

Lesson Assessment

Germany and Brothers Grimm

1. To answer this question, please use your map of the world.
   Where is the continent of Europe located?

2. What continent is Germany on?

3. What separates countries?

4. What did the Brothers Grimm collect?

Student Guide
Lesson 6. Optional: Let's Visit The Netherlands

Lesson Objectives
- Recognize that the country the Netherlands is in Europe.
- Know that people from the Netherlands are called the Dutch.
- Associate the Netherlands with windmills, dikes, and canals.
- Know why dikes are important to the Netherlands.

PREPARE

Approximate lesson time is 45 minutes.

Materials
For the Student
- 🖳 map of Europe
- Mr. Traveler Figurine
- crayons, 16 or more
- pan, baking
- Play-Doh
- popsicle sticks
- water
- 🖳 Flag of the Netherlands
- Hans Brinker: Great Illustrated Classics by Mary Mapes Dodge

Keywords and Pronunciation
canal : A man-made waterway that is sometimes used to carry irrigation water.

dike : A low wall built to hold back water.

windmill : A big, fanlike machine that uses wind power.

LEARN
Activity 1. Optional: Optional Lesson Instructions *(Online)*

This lesson is OPTIONAL. It is provided for students who seek enrichment or extra practice. You may skip this lesson.

If you choose to skip this lesson, then go to the Plan or Lesson Lists page and mark this lesson "Skipped" in order to proceed to the next lesson in the course.

Activity 2. Optional: Traveling with **Mr. Traveler** *(Online)*

Activity 3. Optional: **The Lowlands of Europe** *(Online)*

Activity 4. Optional: **Dikes and Canals** *(Online)*

Activity 5. Optional: **Build a Dike and a Canal** *(Online)*

Activity 6. Optional: **The Little Hero of the Netherlands** *(Online)*

Activity 7. Optional: **The Flag of the Netherlands** *(Online)*

Activity 8. Optional: Ice-Skating on **Canals** *(Online)*

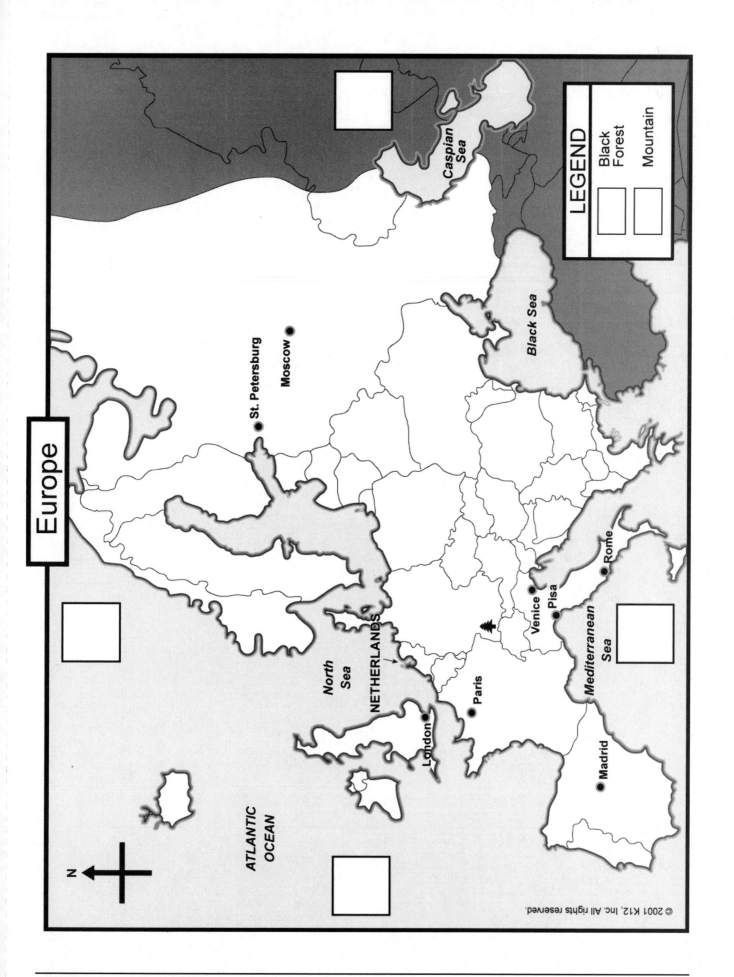

Europe

LEGEND

Black Forest

Mountain

Caspian Sea

Black Sea

Moscow

St. Petersburg

NETHERLANDS

North Sea

Venice

Pisa

Rome

Mediterranean Sea

Paris

London

Madrid

ATLANTIC OCEAN

N

Netherlands

Red	White	Blue

Student Guide
Lesson 7. Optional: Let's Visit Russia

Lesson Objectives

- Associate certain images with Russia, such as onion-domed buildings and Faberge Eggs.
- Identify Russia as being in both Europe and Asia.

PREPARE

Approximate lesson time is 45 minutes.

Materials

For the Student

- 🖥 map of Europe
- food - Onion
- globe, inflatable
- crayons, 16 or more
- 🖥 egg outline
- magazines
- glue sticks
- beads
- glitter
- scissors, round-end safety
- Rechenka's Eggs by Patricia Polacco (ISBN 0698113853)
- 🖥 Flag of Russia

Keywords and Pronunciation

babushka (bah-BOOSH-kuh) : The Russian word for "grandmother."

czar (zahr) : The Russian word for "king."

czarina (zah-REE-nuh) : The wife of the czar.

da (dah) : The Russian word for "yes."

Moskva (muhs-KVAH) : The Russian word for the city of Moscow.

nyet (nyet) : The Russian word for "no."

Peter Carl Faberge (fah-ber-ZHAY)

Peter Tchaikovsky (chiy-KAWF-skee)

Rechenka (RAY-chen-kuh)

Urals (YOUR-uhls)

LEARN
Activity 1. Optional: Optional Lesson Instructions *(Online)*

This lesson is OPTIONAL. It is provided for students who seek enrichment or extra practice. You may skip this lesson.

If you choose to skip this lesson, then go to the Plan or Lesson Lists page and mark this lesson "Skipped" in order to proceed to the next lesson in the course.

Activity 2. Optional: A Country on Two Continents *(Online)*

Activity 3. Optional: Amazing Eggs *(Online)*

Activity 4. Optional: Decorate Your Own Egg *(Online)*

Activity 5. Optional: Reading About Rechenka's Eggs *(Online)*

Activity 6. Optional: The March *(Online)*

Activity 7. Optional: Matryoshka Dolls *(Online)*

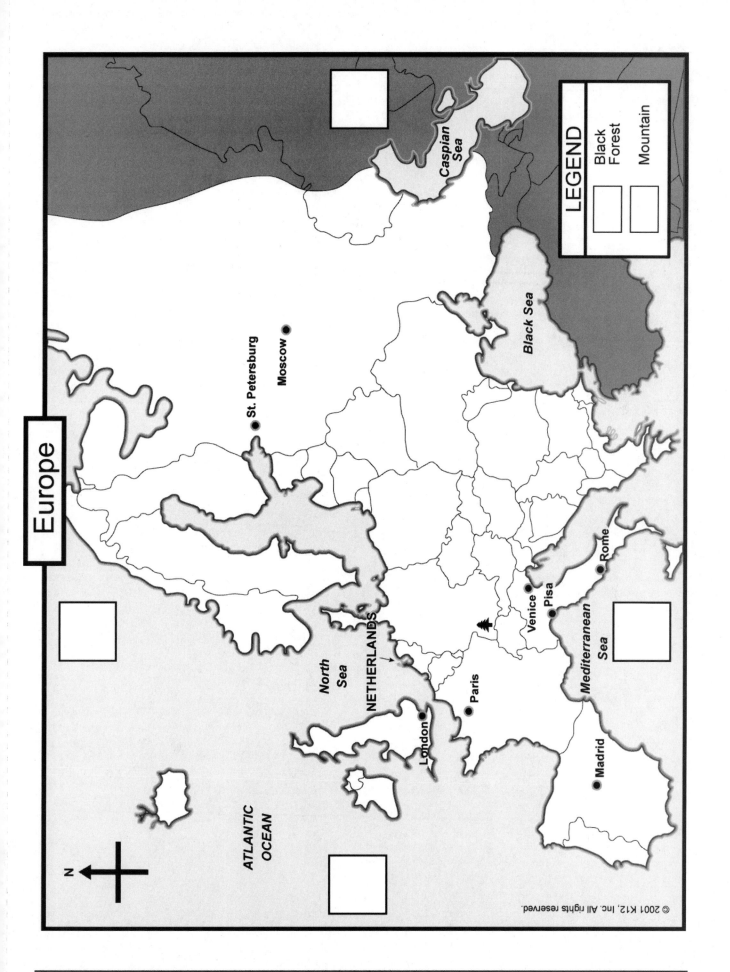

Europe

LEGEND

Black Forest

Mountain

Caspian Sea

Black Sea

St. Petersburg

Moscow

NETHERLANDS

North Sea

Venice

Pisa

Rome

Mediterranean Sea

Paris

London

Madrid

ATLANTIC OCEAN

N

Russia

White

Blue

Red

Student Guide
Lesson 8: Let's Visit Italy and Wave Good-bye to Europe

Lesson Objectives

- Recognize that Italy is in Europe.
- With assistance, locate previously studied countries in Europe on a map.
- Use the cardinal directions to move from one European country to the next.

PREPARE

Approximate lesson time is 45 minutes.

Materials

For the Student

    📖 map of Europe

    globe, inflatable

    Mr. Traveler Figurine

    map, world

    📖 flag of Italy

    crayons, 16 or more

    📖 Review Questions

    pencils, no. 2

    string

    tape, clear

Optional

    📖 Postcard backs

    📖 Postcard fronts

    glue sticks

    postage stamps

    index cards, 4" x 6"

    pencils, colored, 16 or more

    scissors, round-end safety

    Big Anthony and the Magic Ring by Tomie dePaola

    Big Anthony: His Story by Tomie dePaola

    Strega Nona by Tomie dePaola

    Strega Nona Meets Her Match by Tomie dePaola

    Strega Nona's Magic Lessons by Tomie dePaola

Keywords and Pronunciation

ciao (chow) : The Italian word for "hello" and "good-bye."

globe : A model of Earth.

gondola (GAHN-duh-luh) : A wooden boat used on canals in Italy.

gondolas (GAHN-duh-luhs)

Leonardo da Vinci (lay-uh-NAHR-doh duh VIN-chee)

Mediterranean (med-uh-tuh-RAY-nee-uhn)

peninsula : A piece of land that sticks out and is almost surrounded by water.

Pisa (PEE-zuh)

ruin : The remains of an ancient building.

Strega Nona (STRAY-guh NOH-nuh)

LEARN
Activity 1: Traveling Through Europe *(Online)*

Activity 2: Welcome to Italy *(Online)*

Activity 3: Seeing the Sights *(Online)*

Activity 4: Flag Fun *(Online)*

Activity 5: Putting It All Together *(Online)*

Activity 6. Optional: Postcards--Looking Back at Europe *(Online)*

ASSESS

Lesson Assessment: Let's Visit Italy and Wave Good-bye to Europe (*Online*)
You will complete an offline assessment covering the main objectives of this lesson. Your learning coach will score this assessment.

LEARN
Activity 7. Optional: Read On *(Online)*

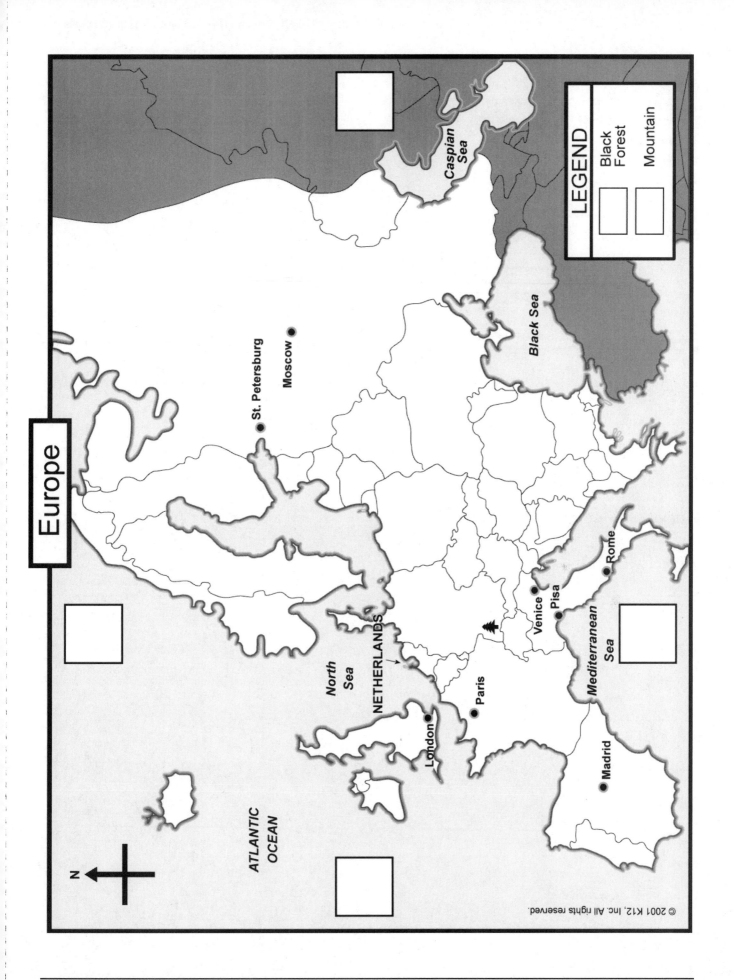

Europe

LEGEND

Black Forest

Mountain

Caspian Sea

Black Sea

St. Petersburg

Moscow

NETHERLANDS

North Sea

Paris

London

Venice

Pisa

Rome

Mediterranean Sea

Madrid

ATLANTIC OCEAN

N

Red

White

Green

Italy

Europe Review Questions

There are four questions for each country. Read the first question for a country. If your student answers incorrectly, read the next question for that country. Stick with one country until your student gets it right. Review all the questions under one country before going on to the next country.

Questions for Spain
1. In which country can you watch a bullfight?
2. In which country will you find a city called Madrid that once was surrounded by a thick stone wall?
3. Which country is separated from France by the Pyrenees Mountains?
4. Cork trees grow in which country?

Questions for England
1. Which country once had a bridge called London Bridge that was falling down?
2. Which country has a river called the River Thames that runs right through the city of London?
3. Which country has a big clock called Big Ben attached to a building called the Palace of Westminster?
4. Which country has soldiers wearing tall fur hats standing guard in front of Buckingham Palace?

Questions for France
1. In which country will you see the Eiffel Tower?
2. Which country is separated from Spain by the Pyrenees Mountains?
3. Which country has a huge church called the Cathedral of Notre Dame that has stone gargoyles sitting on the ledges?
4. The song *Frère Jacques* comes from what country?

Questions for Ireland
1. Which country is nicknamed the Emerald Isle?
2. Leprechauns and giants come from which country?
3. A green shamrock should remind you of which country?
4. Which country tells the legend of Finn McCool?

Questions for Germany
1. In what country did Jacob and Wilhelm Grimm grow up? (Hint: the fairytale authors)
2. In what country will you find Neuschwanstein Castle? (Hint: it looks like the castle at Walt Disney World)
3. The Black Forest, often found in fairytales, is in what country?
4. In what country do they say *ja* for "yes" and *nein* for "no"?

Europe Review Questions

OPTIONAL: Questions for the Netherlands
    1. Which country has dikes and canals?
    2. The name of which country actually means "low lands"?
    3. In what country will you find windmills pumping water back into the sea?
    4. Dutch people live in what country?

OPTIONAL: Questions for Russia
    1. Fabergé Eggs were made in what country?
    2. In what country do people call the king and queen the czar and the czarina?
    3. Which country has buildings with onion-shaped tops?
    4. In which country do children call their grandmothers "babushkas"?

Europe: Many Countries, Many Stories   Let's Visit Italy and Wave Good-bye to Europe

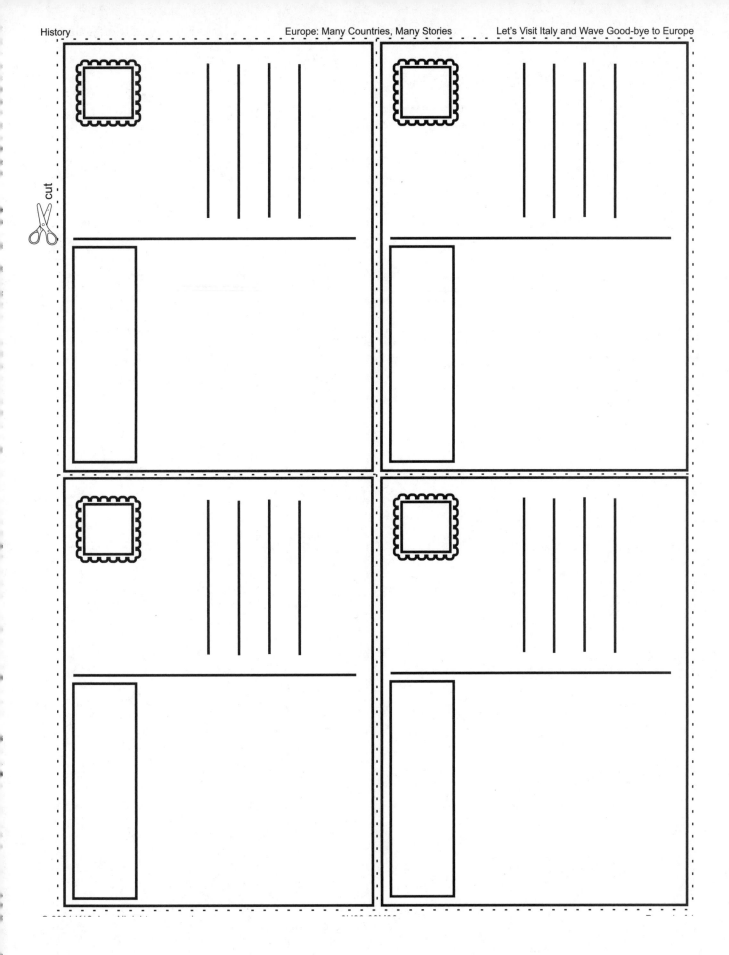

cut

cut

cut

Lesson Assessment

Let's Visit Italy and Wave Good-bye to Europe

1. To answer this question, please use your map of the world.
   Where is the country of Spain located?

2. To answer this question, please use your map of the world.
   Which direction would you be traveling if you went from Ireland to England?

3. What continent is Italy a part of?

Student Guide
Lesson 1: Slow Boat Through China

Explore the diverse regions, people, and legends of a vast continent. Travel down the great rivers of China, and visit the densely populated islands of Japan. Then it's off to India's Taj Mahal and a final stop on the Arabian peninsula.

Lesson Objectives

- Identify China as a country in Asia.
- Know that the Yangtze River is an important river in China.
- Locate Asia on a globe.
- Locate Russia on a map of Asia.

PREPARE

Approximate lesson time is 45 minutes.

Materials

For the Student

- map of Asia
- globe, inflatable
- Mr. Traveler Figurine
- paper, colored construction, 12"x12"
- crayons, 16 or more
- Suitcase Cover
- folder, manila
- Elmer's Glue-All
- stapler
- Dragon Head activity sheet
- glue sticks
- ruler, standard 12"
- scissors, round-end safety
- The Story About Ping by Marjorie Flack (ISBN 0140502416)

Optional

- Memory Book Pages
- chopsticks
- The Donkey and the Rock by Demi
- The Empty Pot by Demi

Keywords and Pronunciation
long chuan (lohng chwahn)
ni hao (nee how)
Yangtze (YANG-see)

LEARN
Activity 1: The Largest Continent *(Online)*

Activity 2: Traveling to China *(Online)*

Activity 3: Create a Dragon Boat *(Online)*

Activity 4: Up the Yangtze River *(Online)*

Activity 5: Read Aloud - The Story About Ping *(Online)*

Activity 6. Optional: Memory Book *(Online)*

ASSESS

Lesson Assessment: Slow Boat Through China (*Online*)

You will complete an offline assessment covering the main objectives of this lesson. Your learning coach will score this assessment.

LEARN
Activity 7. Optional: Try Your Hand at Chopsticks *(Online)*

Activity 8. Optional: Read On *(Online)*

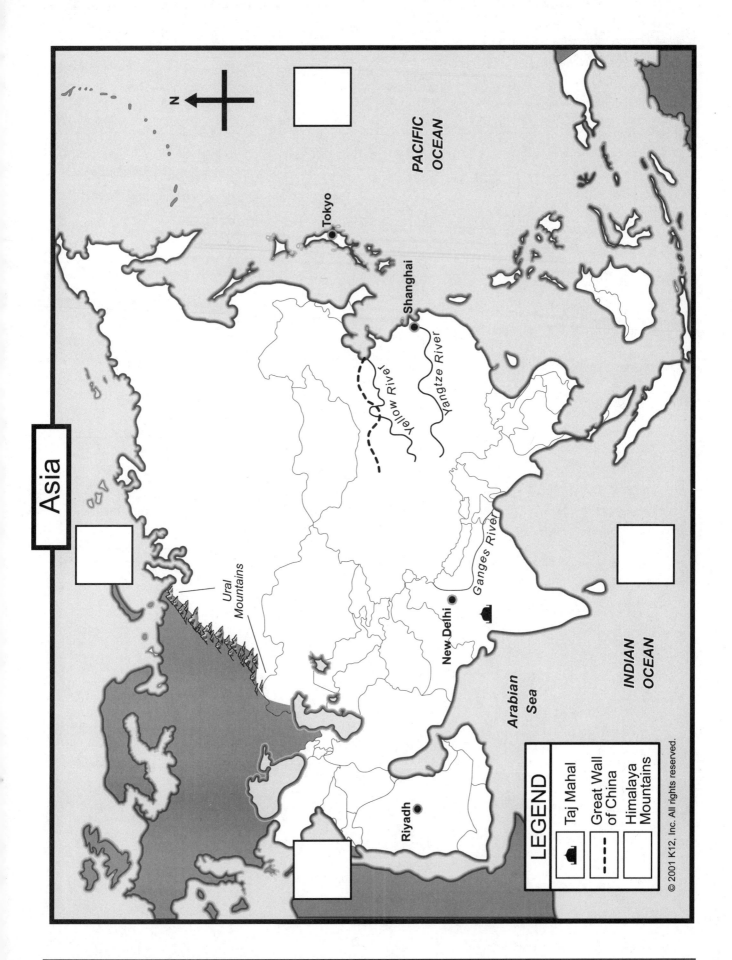

Asia

N

PACIFIC OCEAN

Tokyo

Shanghai

Yellow River

Yangtze River

Ganges River

Ural Mountains

New Delhi

Arabian Sea

INDIAN OCEAN

Riyadh

LEGEND

Taj Mahal

Great Wall of China

Himalaya Mountains

© 2001 K12, Inc. All rights reserved.

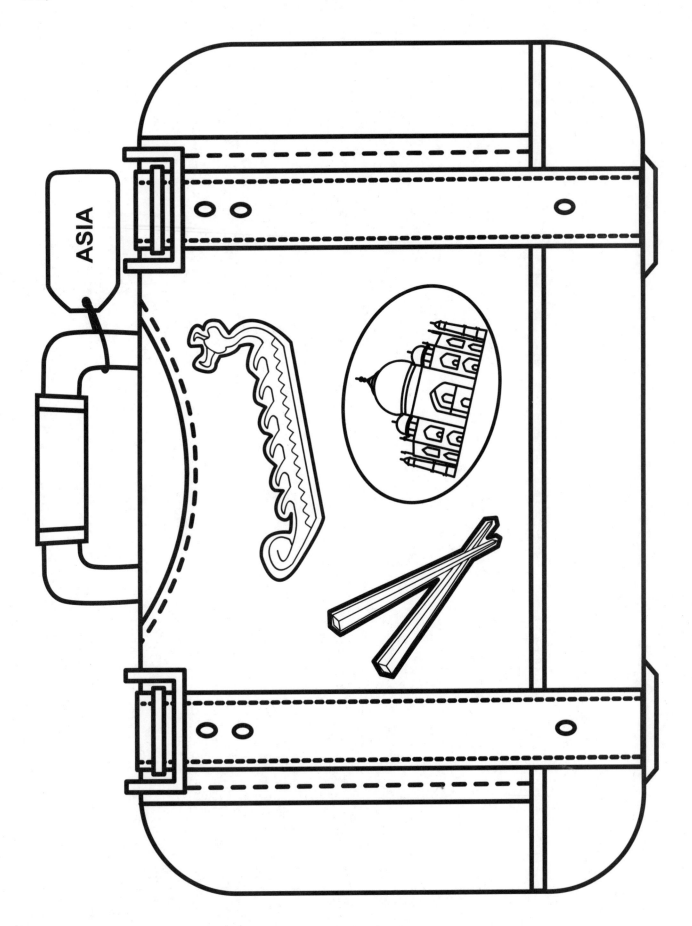

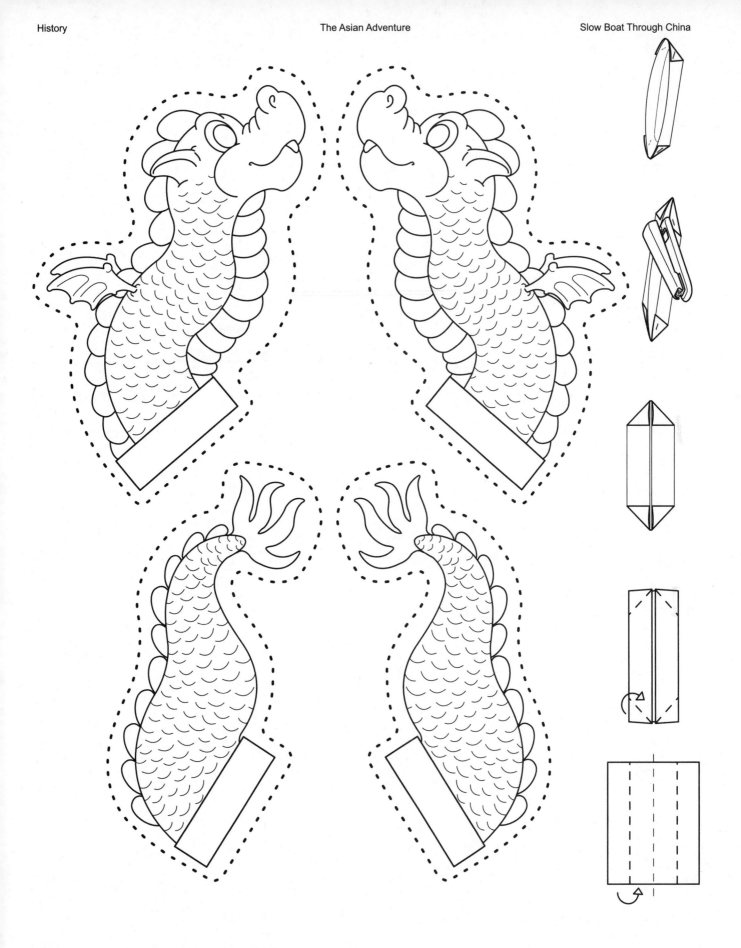

Shanghai, China

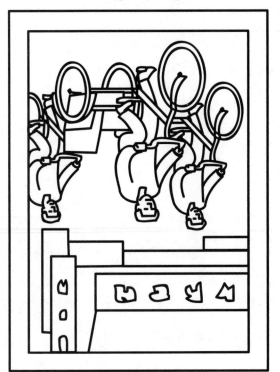

Himalaya Mountains

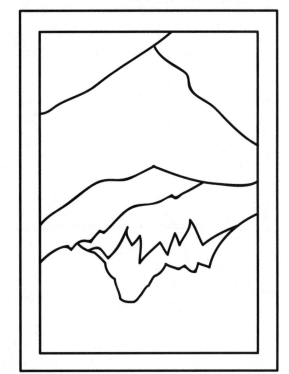

My Memory Book of China

The Dragon Boat Festival on the Yangtze River

Rice Fields and Paddies

Lesson Assessment

Slow Boat Through China

1. To answer this question, please use your globe.
   Where is the continent of Asia located?

2. To answer this question, please use the map of Asia.
   Where is the country of Russia located?

3. To answer this question, please use the map of Asia.
   Where is the country of China located?

4. Is the Yangtze an important river in China?

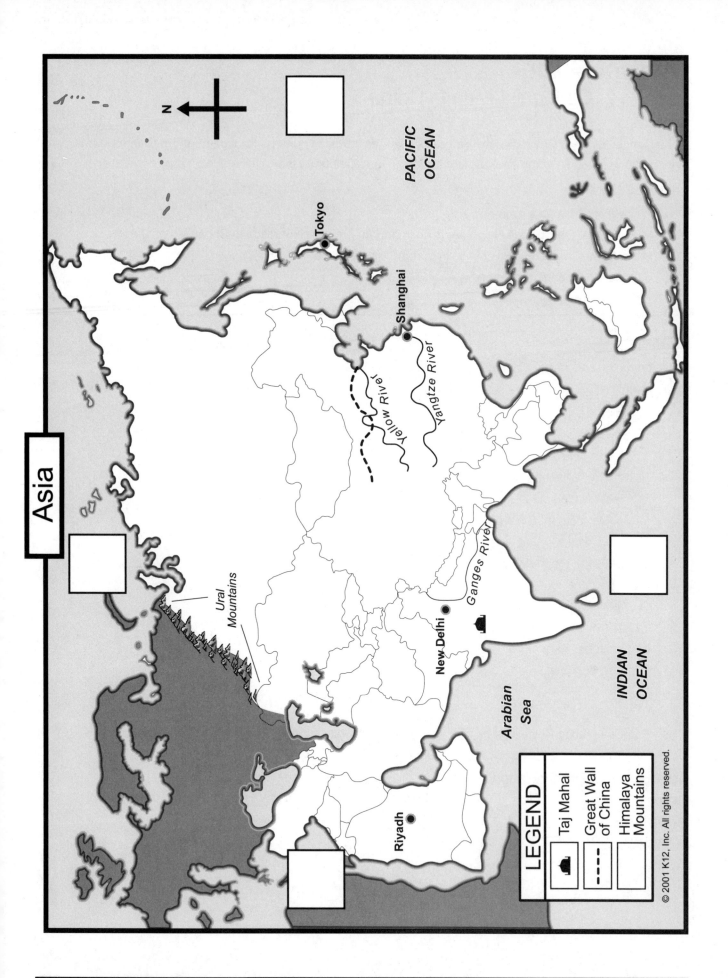

Asia

N

PACIFIC
OCEAN

Tokyo

Shanghai

Yellow River

Yangtze River

Ganges River

Ural
Mountains

New Delhi

INDIAN
OCEAN

Arabian
Sea

Riyadh

Student Guide
Lesson 2. Optional: Living in China

Get a glimpse of life in China. Follow the Yellow River as it twists and turns through northern China. Hear a legend about the origin of the Yangtze and Yellow Rivers. Celebrate the Chinese New Year.

Lesson Objectives

- Identify China as a country in Asia.
- Know that the Chinese New Year is an important holiday celebration in China.
- Know that the Yellow River is an important river in China.
- Locate Asia on a world map.

PREPARE

Approximate lesson time is 45 minutes.

Materials

For the Student

- 🖥 Chinese Zodiac sheet
- 🖥 map of Asia
- 🖥 Red Envelope pattern
- globe, inflatable
- paper, colored construction, 12"x12"
- map, world
- scissors, round-end safety
- tape, clear
- stapler
- 🖥 Chinese Zodiac
- crayons, 16 or more
- plates, paper
- paper clips
- string
- Celebrating Chinese New Year by Diane Hoyt-Goldsmith
- The Dancing Dragon by Marcia Vaughan

Keywords and Pronunciation

Fu (foo)

Huang (hwahng)

Jinsha (jing-shah)

LEARN
Activity 1. Optional: Optional Lesson Instructions *(Online)*

This lesson is OPTIONAL. It is provided for students who seek enrichment or extra practice. You may skip this lesson.

If you choose to skip this lesson, then go to the Plan or Lesson Lists page and mark this lesson "Skipped" in order to proceed to the next lesson in the course.

Activity 2. Optional: Finding Asia *(Online)*

Activity 3. Optional: A Trip Down the Yellow River *(Online)*

Activity 4. Optional: The Tale of the Two Dragons *(Online)*

Activity 5. Optional: Make a Chinese New Year's Lantern *(Online)*

Activity 6. Optional: Celebrate the Chinese New Year *(Online)*

Activity 7. Optional: The Chinese Zodiac *(Online)*

Activity 8. Optional: Make a Dragon Puppet *(Online)*

Activity 9. Optional: Read On *(Online)*

Red Envelope Pattern

Create an envelope out of red construction paper using the following directions. Place the Chinese Zodiac Sheet inside the envelope, tape shut, and set aside for use later in the lesson.

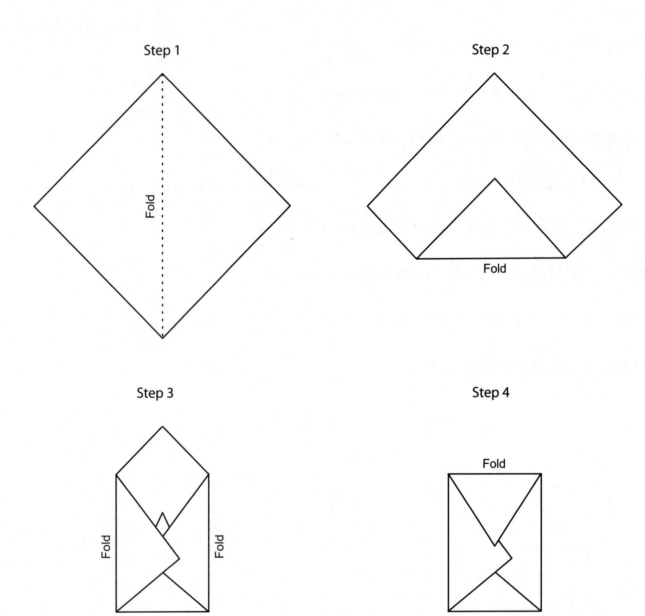

Step 1

Step 2

Step 3

Step 4

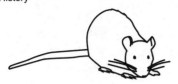

The Rat

1900, 1912, 1924, 1936, 1948, 1960, 1972, 1984, 1996, 2008, 2020
You are charming, fun, and very easy to get along with.
You work hard and save your money, but are generous
with those people you really like.

The Ox

1901, 1913, 1925, 1937, 1949, 1961, 1973, 1985, 1997, 2009, 2021
You are very hardworking and dependable, and these qualities will bring
you good fortune. You are a good listener and very fair to everyone.
People find you easy to trust.

The Tiger

1902, 1914, 1926, 1938, 1950, 1962, 1974, 1986, 1998, 2010, 2022
You have an exciting personality and are prepared for everything that
comes your way. You love life and love to be the center of attention.

The Rabbit

1903, 1915, 1927, 1939, 1951, 1963, 1975, 1987, 1999, 2011, 2023
You are very kind and have good manners. Your good judgment,
thoughtfulness, and artistic ability will help you lead a peaceful life.

The Dragon

1904, 1916, 1928, 1940, 1952, 1964, 1976, 1988, 2000, 2012, 2024
You are very energetic and strong, constantly on the go. People are
drawn to your energy, and you will always have a lot of admirers.

The Snake

1905, 1917, 1929, 1941, 1953, 1965, 1977, 1989, 2001, 2013, 2025
You are a deep thinker and love good books and beautiful things. You
should trust yourself to make good decisions throughout your life.

The Horse

1906, 1918, 1930, 1942, 1954, 1966, 1978, 1990, 2002, 2014, 2026
You are cheerful, popular, and have a good sense of humor. You have the ability to make quick decisions, and you like to have different ideas from those of other people.

The Sheep

1907, 1919, 1931, 1943, 1955, 1967, 1979, 1991, 2003, 2015, 2027
You are very sensitive and creative. People like you because you are kind and forgive easily. You may be good at a job working with children or animals.

The Monkey

1908, 1920, 1932, 1944, 1956, 1968, 1980, 1992, 2004, 2016, 2028
You have a quick mind and are good at inventing things. You are a very fast learner and have a talent for learning languages.

The Rooster

1909, 1921, 1933, 1945, 1957, 1969, 1981, 1993, 2005, 2017, 2029
You are very neat and organized, and you are good at saying what you mean. You like to show people how smart you are and would be good at a career in the public eye.

The Dog

1910, 1922, 1934, 1946, 1958, 1970, 1982, 1994, 2006, 2018, 2030
You are honest and intelligent, and you like everything to be fair for everyone. You are a very good friend and always help those in need. People find you easy to like.

The Boar

1911, 1923, 1935, 1947, 1959, 1971, 1983, 1995, 2007, 2019, 2031
You are a very sensitive person and a perfect friend to others. You may not like to handle money, but fortune will always be around you.

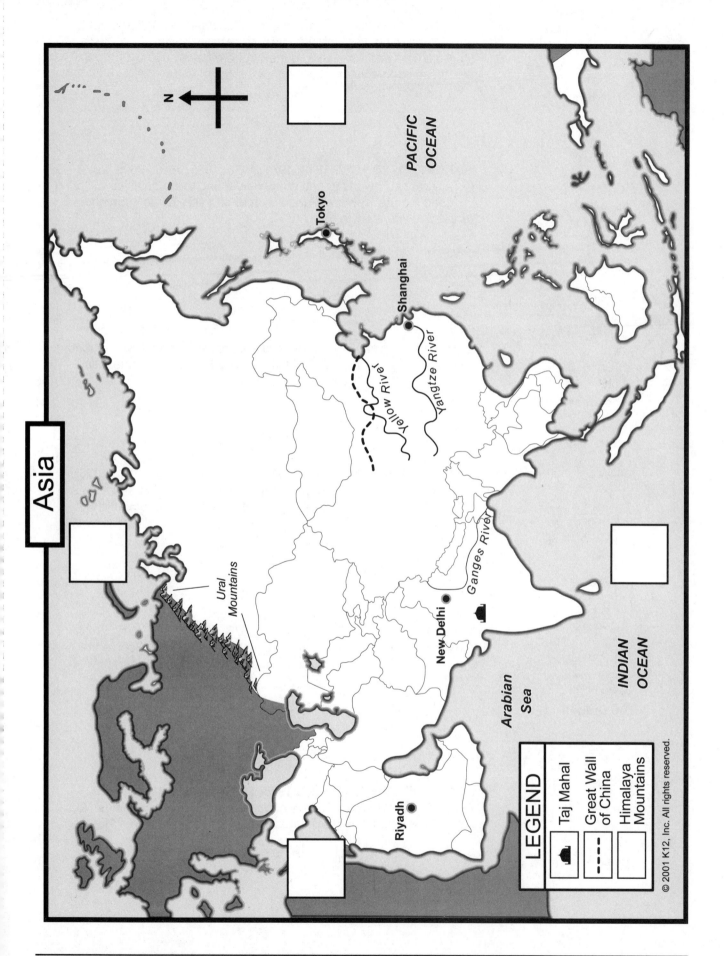

Asia

N

PACIFIC
OCEAN

Tokyo

Shanghai

Yellow River

Yangtze River

Ganges River

Ural
Mountains

New Delhi

Arabian
Sea

INDIAN
OCEAN

Riyadh

LEGEND

Taj Mahal

Great Wall
of China

Himalaya
Mountains

© 2001 K12, Inc. All rights reserved.

The Rat

1900, 1912, 1924, 1936, 1948, 1960, 1972, 1984, 1996, 2008, 2020
You are charming, fun, and very easy to get along with.
You work hard and save your money, but are generous
with those people you really like.

The Ox

1901, 1913, 1925, 1937, 1949, 1961, 1973, 1985, 1997, 2009, 2021
You are very hardworking and dependable, and these qualities will bring
you good fortune. You are a good listener and very fair to everyone.
People find you easy to trust.

The Tiger

1902, 1914, 1926, 1938, 1950, 1962, 1974, 1986, 1998, 2010, 2022
You have an exciting personality and are prepared for everything that
comes your way. You love life and love to be the center of attention.

The Rabbit

1903, 1915, 1927, 1939, 1951, 1963, 1975, 1987, 1999, 2011, 2023
You are very kind and have good manners. Your good judgment,
thoughtfulness, and artistic ability will help you lead a peaceful life.

The Dragon

1904, 1916, 1928, 1940, 1952, 1964, 1976, 1988, 2000, 2012, 2024
You are very energetic and strong, constantly on the go. People are
drawn to your energy, and you will always have a lot of admirers.

The Snake

1905, 1917, 1929, 1941, 1953, 1965, 1977, 1989, 2001, 2013, 2025
You are a deep thinker and love good books and beautiful things. You
should trust yourself to make good decisions throughout your life.

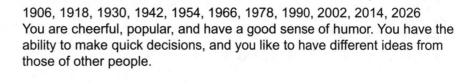

The Horse

1906, 1918, 1930, 1942, 1954, 1966, 1978, 1990, 2002, 2014, 2026
You are cheerful, popular, and have a good sense of humor. You have the ability to make quick decisions, and you like to have different ideas from those of other people.

The Sheep

1907, 1919, 1931, 1943, 1955, 1967, 1979, 1991, 2003, 2015, 2027
You are very sensitive and creative. People like you because you are kind and forgive easily. You may be good at a job working with children or animals.

The Monkey

1908, 1920, 1932, 1944, 1956, 1968, 1980, 1992, 2004, 2016, 2028
You have a quick mind and are good at inventing things. You are a very fast learner and have a talent for learning languages.

The Rooster

1909, 1921, 1933, 1945, 1957, 1969, 1981, 1993, 2005, 2017, 2029
You are very neat and organized, and you are good at saying what you mean. You like to show people how smart you are and would be good at a career in the public eye.

The Dog

1910, 1922, 1934, 1946, 1958, 1970, 1982, 1994, 2006, 2018, 2030
You are honest and intelligent, and you like everything to be fair for everyone. You are a very good friend and always help those in need. People find you easy to like.

The Boar

1911, 1923, 1935, 1947, 1959, 1971, 1983, 1995, 2007, 2019, 2031
You are a very sensitive person and a perfect friend to others. You may not like to handle money, but fortune will always be around you.

Student Guide
Lesson 3: A Tour of Japan

Lesson Objectives

- Identify Tokyo and Mount Fuji as places in Japan.
- Know that Japan is made up of islands.
- Know that Japan is a country in Asia.

PREPARE

Approximate lesson time is 45 minutes.

Materials

For the Student

- map of Asia
- globe, inflatable
- crayons, 16 or more
- Mr. Traveler Figurine
- Fish Pattern
- bags, brown paper grocery
- Elmer's Glue-All
- markers, colored, 8 or more
- paper, 8 1/2" x 11" (2)
- scissors, round-end safety
- string

Optional

- O-bento Lunch box pattern
- box, shirt-size
- paper, colored construction, 12"x12" - any color
- How My Parents Learned to Eat by Ina R. Friedman

Keywords and Pronunciation

Bunraku (bun-RAH-koo)

Fuji (FOO-jee)

futon (FOO-tahn)

konichiwa (koh-NEE-chee-wah)

Mutsumi (moo-TSOO-mee)

o-bento (oh-BEN-toh)

sayonara (siy-oh-NAH-ruh)

shoji (SHOH-jee)

sushi (SOO-shee)

LEARN
Activity 1: Map Review *(Online)*

Activity 2: Introduction to Japan *(Online)*

Activity 3: Make a Fish Kite *(Online)*

Activity 4: Touring the Islands *(Online)*

Activity 5. Optional: A Japanese Lunchbox *(Online)*

ASSESS

Lesson Assessment: A Tour of Japan (*Online*)

You will complete an offline assessment covering the main objectives of this lesson. Your learning coach will score this assessment.

LEARN
Activity 6. Optional: Suggested Reading *(Online)*

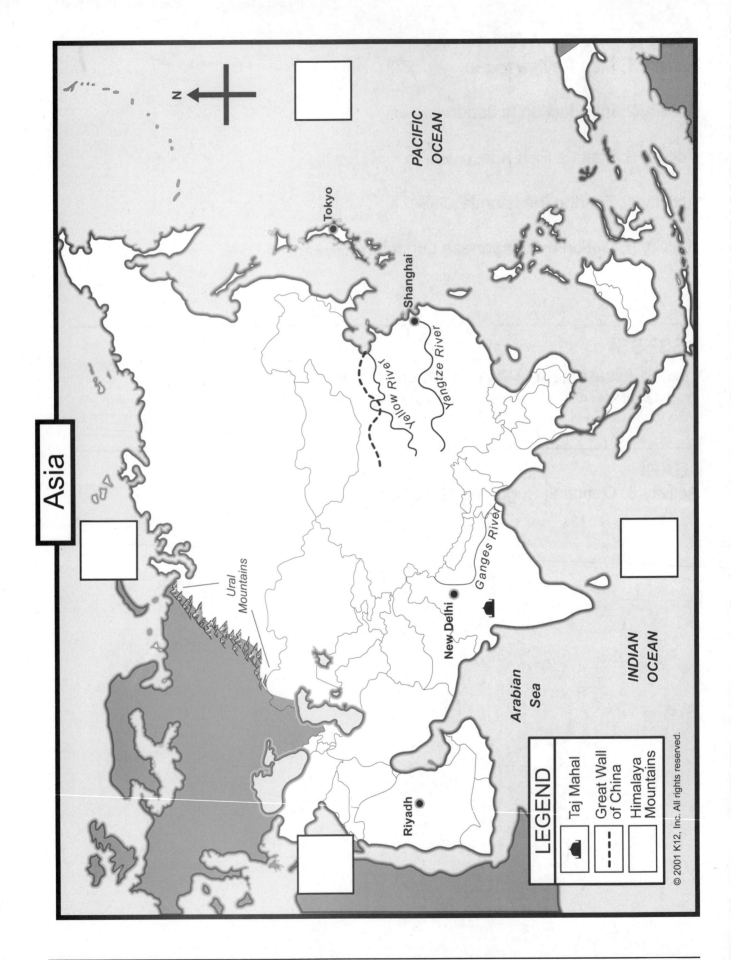

Asia

PACIFIC OCEAN

Tokyo

Shanghai

Yellow River

Yangtze River

Ganges River

New Delhi

Ural Mountains

INDIAN OCEAN

Arabian Sea

Riyadh

LEGEND
Taj Mahal
Great Wall of China
Himalaya Mountains

158

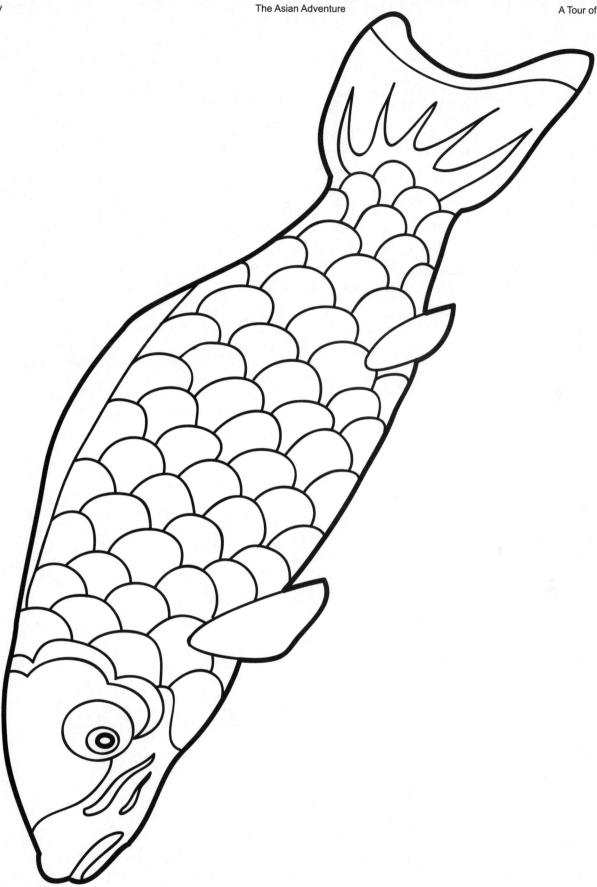

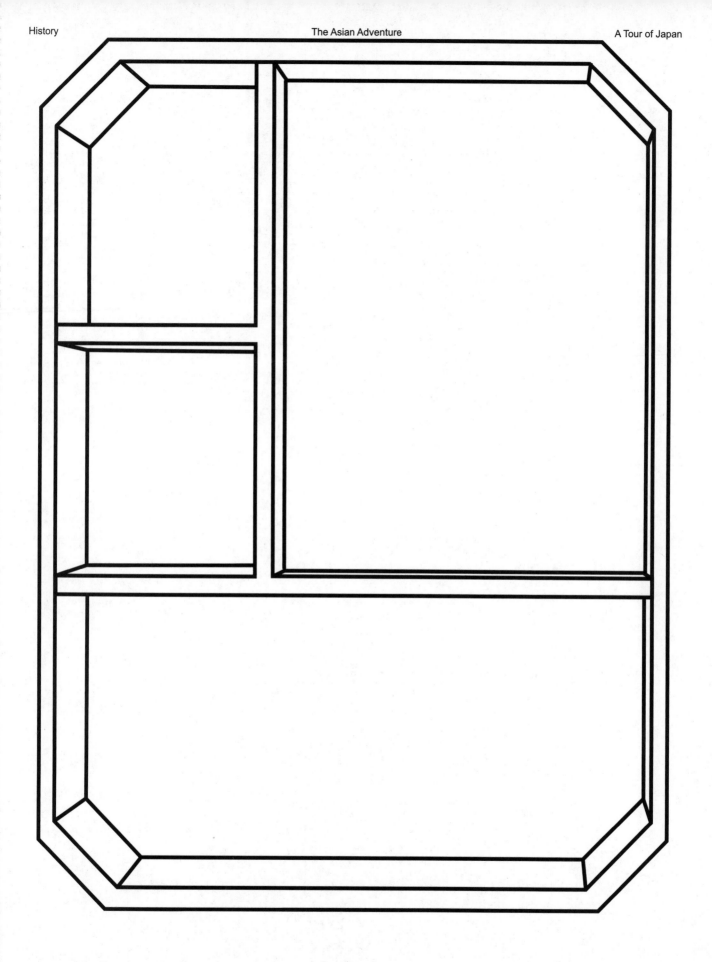

Lesson Assessment

A Tour of Japan

1. What continent is Japan a part of?

2. What type of land is Japan made up of?

3. Both of these places-Tokyo and Mount Fuji-are located in which country?

Student Guide
Lesson 4. Optional: Japan: Of Peaches and Puppets

Lesson Objectives

- Recognize Japan as a country in Asia that is made up of islands.
- Know that Momotaro, or Peach Boy, is a favorite tale from Japan.

PREPARE

Approximate lesson time is 45 minutes.

Materials

For the Student

    📖 map of Asia

    📖 Peach Boy activity sheet

    crayons, 16 or more

    paper, colored construction, 12"x12"

    Elmer's Glue-All

    popsicle sticks (7)

    scissors, round-end safety

    sheet

    household items - table

    paints, watercolor, 8 colors or more

    stapler

    tape, clear

Keywords and Pronunciation

konichiwa (koh-NEE-chee-wah)

Momotaro (moh-moh-TAR-oh)

LEARN
Activity 1. Optional: Optional Lesson Instructions *(Online)*

This lesson is OPTIONAL. It is provided for students who seek enrichment or extra practice. You may skip this lesson.

If you choose to skip this lesson, then go to the Plan or Lesson Lists page and mark this lesson "Skipped" in order to proceed to the next lesson in the course.

Activity 2. Optional: Map Fact Review *(Online)*

Activity 3. Optional: Momotaro, Peach Boy *(Online)*

Activity 4. Optional: Making Puppets *(Online)*

Activity 5. Optional: Puppet Theater *(Online)*

Activity 6. Optional: Make a Fan *(Online)*

Activity 7. Optional: Daruma *(Online)*

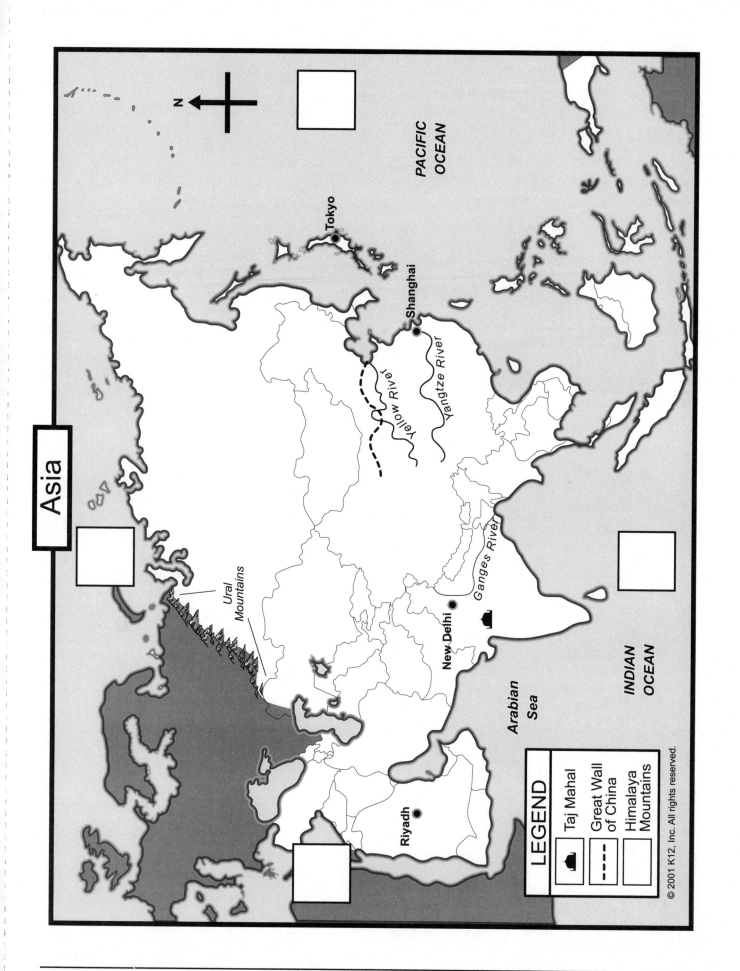

Asia

PACIFIC
OCEAN

Tokyo

Shanghai

Yellow River

Yangtze River

Ganges River

Ural
Mountains

New Delhi

Arabian
Sea

INDIAN
OCEAN

Riyadh

LEGEND

Taj Mahal

Great Wall
of China

Himalaya
Mountains

© 2001 K12, Inc. All rights reserved.

167

Momotaro the Peach Boy Puppets

cut

Student Guide
Lesson 5: Into India

Lesson Objectives

- Identify the Ganges as a river in India
- Locate India on a map of Asia.
- Locate the Himalaya Mountains on the map of Asia.
- Recognize India as a country in Asia.

PREPARE

Approximate lesson time is 45 minutes.

Materials

For the Student

- map of Asia
- Mr. Traveler Figurine
- crayons, 16 or more
- pencils, no. 2
- Indian elephant coloring sheet

Optional

- Taj Mahal picture
- Elmer's Glue-All
- household items - spices
- elastic thread
- small jingle bells
- beads
- scissors, round-end safety

Keywords and Pronunciation

Ganges (GAN-jeez)
Himalayas (hih-muh-LAY-uhz)
minarets (min-uh-RETS)
sitars (SIH-tarz)
Taj Mahal (tahj mah-HAHL)

LEARN
Activity 1: Review of Travel in China and Japan *(Online)*

Activity 2: Traveling to India *(Online)*

Activity 3: The Taj Mahal *(Online)*

Activity 4: Color an Indian Elephant *(Online)*

Activity 5: The Blind Men and the Elephant *(Online)*

Activity 6. Optional: Spices of India *(Online)*

ASSESS

Lesson Assessment: Into India (*Online*)
You will complete an offline assessment covering the main objectives of this lesson. Your learning coach will score this assessment.

LEARN
Activity 7. Optional: Indian Music *(Online)*

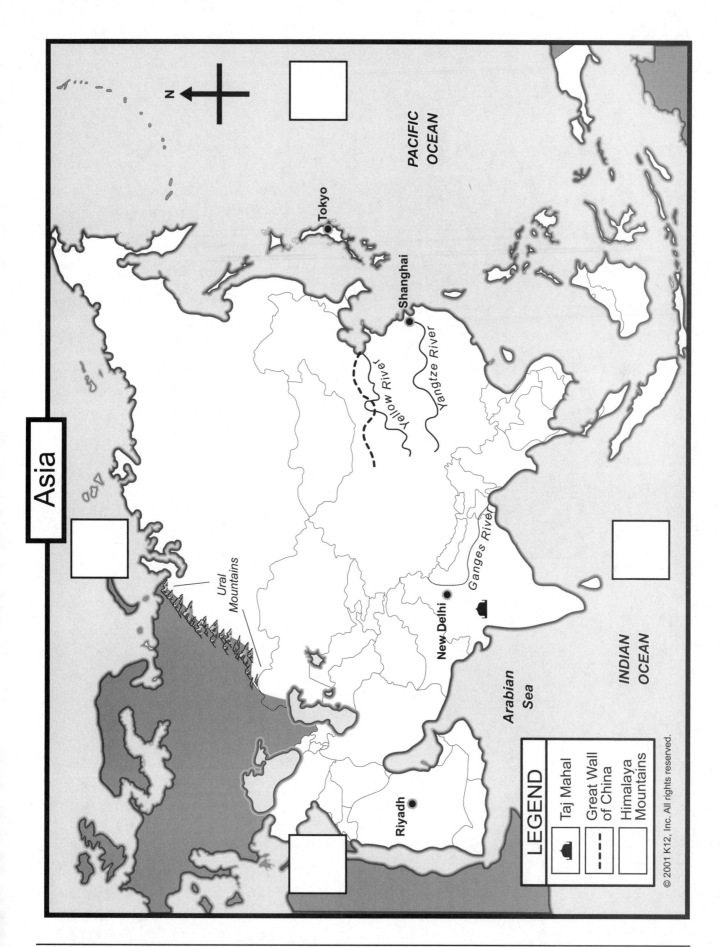

Asia

PACIFIC
OCEAN

Tokyo

Shanghai

Yellow River

Yangtze River

Ganges River

Ural
Mountains

New Delhi

INDIAN
OCEAN

Arabian
Sea

Riyadh

LEGEND

◼	Taj Mahal
╎	Great Wall of China
☐	Himalaya Mountains

Lesson Assessment

Into India

1. To answer this question, please use your map of Asia. Where is the country of India?

2. On what continent do we find India?

3. Located in India, what is the Ganges?

4. To answer this question, please use your map of Asia. Where are the Himalaya Mountains located?

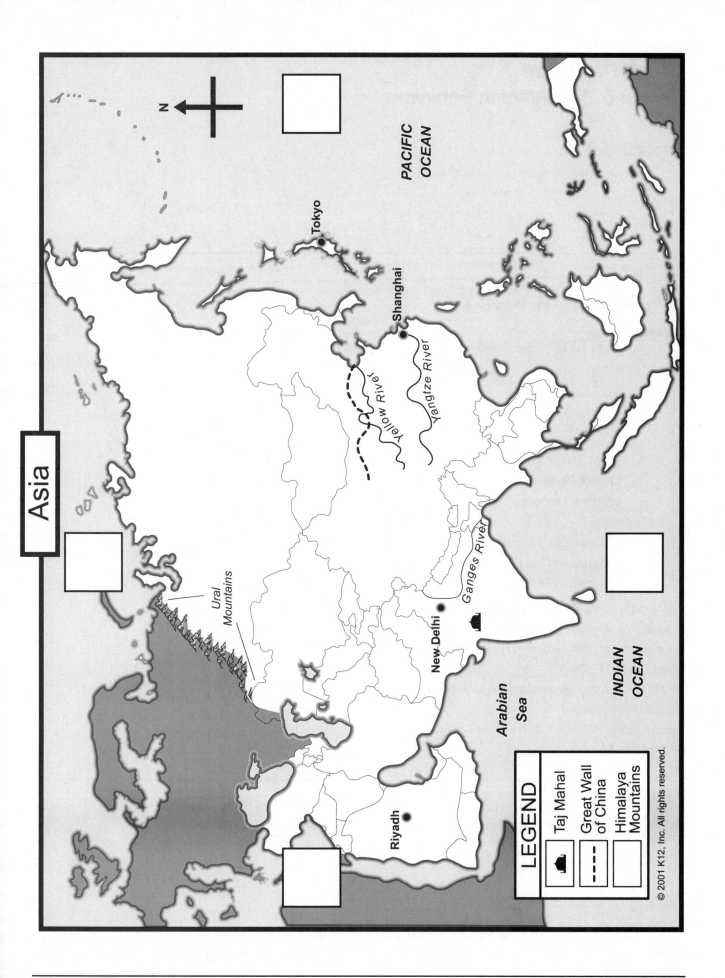

Asia

PACIFIC OCEAN

N

Tokyo

Shanghai

Yellow River

Yangtze River

Ural Mountains

Ganges River

New Delhi

INDIAN OCEAN

Arabian Sea

Riyadh

LEGEND

Taj Mahal

Great Wall of China

Himalaya Mountains

Student Guide
Lesson 6: The Arabian Peninsula

Lesson Objectives

- Locate Saudi Arabia on a map of Asia.
- Identify Saudi Arabia as a peninsula.
- Summarize the story of Sinbad and the Roc.

PREPARE

Approximate lesson time is 45 minutes.

Materials

For the Student

- 🖥 map of Asia

   crayons, 16 or more

   Mr. Traveler Figurine

- 🖥 The Roc activity sheet

   paper, colored construction, 12"x12"

   Elmer's Glue-All

   scissors, round-end safety

Optional

- 🖥 Asia activity sheet

   Ali Baba and the Forty Thieves retold by Margaret Early

   The Tale of Ali Baba and the Forty Thieves retold by Eric A. Kimmel

Keywords and Pronunciation

Al salaam a alaykum (ah sah-LAHM ah ah-LAY-koom)

eucalyp : A dry area, usually covered with sand.

Fareed (fah-REED)

ghutra (GOO-trah) : A square cloth folded into a triangle and worn by Arabs as a protective head covering.

Riyadh (REE-yahd)

Saudi Arabia (SAW-dee uh-RAY-bee-uh)

Sayeed (siy-EED)

LEARN
Activity 1: Geography *(Online)*

Activity 2: Living in Saudi Arabia *(Online)*

Activity 3: Wearing a Ghutra *(Online)*

Activity 4: Sinbad and the Roc *(Online)*

Activity 5: Coloring Roc *(Online)*

Activity 6: Tic Tac Go *(Online)*

Activity 7. Optional: Review of Asia *(Online)*

ASSESS

Lesson Assessment: The Arabian Peninsula (*Online*)

You will complete an offline assessment covering the main objectives of this lesson. Your learning coach will score this assessment.

LEARN

Activity 8. Optional: Read About Ali Baba *(Online)*

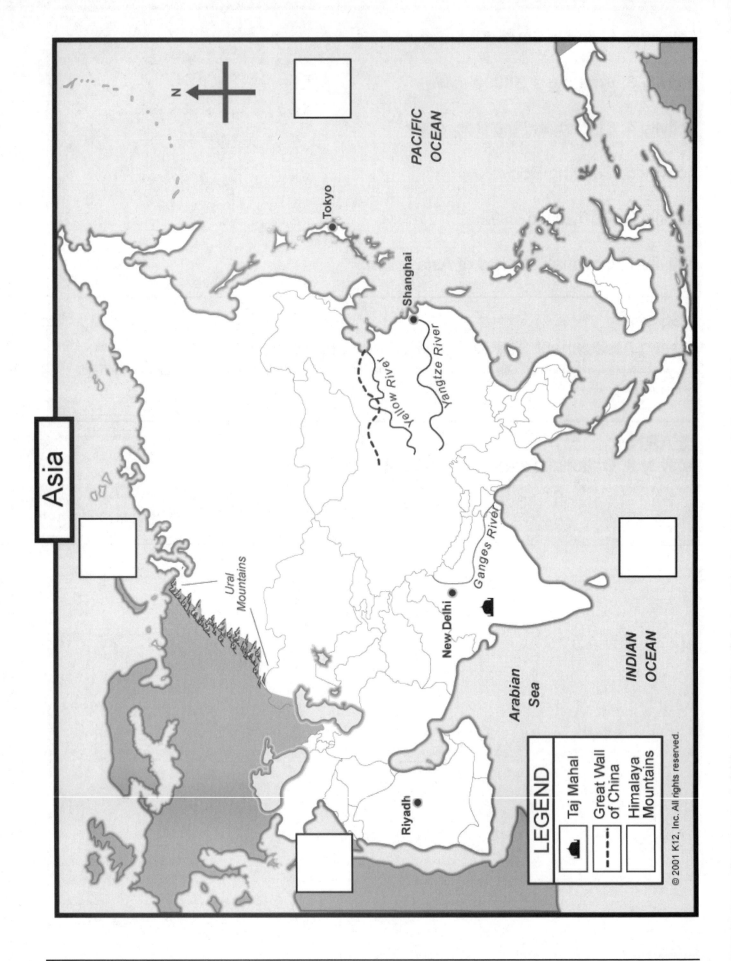

Asia

N

PACIFIC OCEAN

Tokyo

Shanghai

Yellow River

Yangtze River

Ganges River

Ural Mountains

New Delhi

INDIAN OCEAN

Arabian Sea

Riyadh

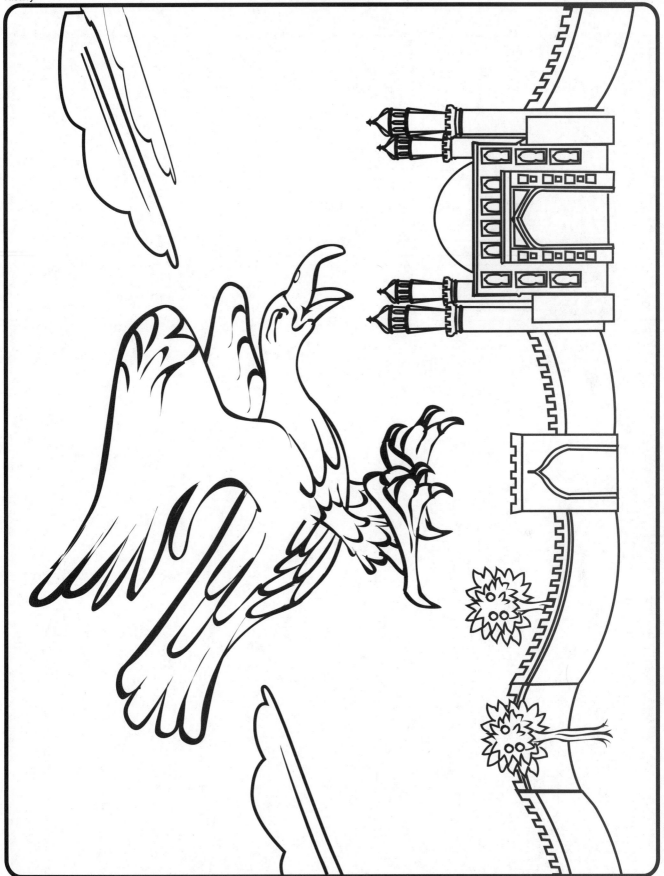

cut

The Great Wall
of China

Chinese Pandas

Japanese Fish Kite

Mount Fuji, Japan

The Taj Mahal, India

Indian Elephant

Camels in Saudi
Arabia

Saudi Arabian
Ghutra

Lesson Assessment

The Arabian Peninsula

1. To answer this question, please use your map of Asia.
   Where is the country of Saudia Arabia?

2. What can you recall of the story of Sinbad and the Roc?

3. Saudia Arabia sticks out into the water and almost all of the country is surrounded by water. What is this called?

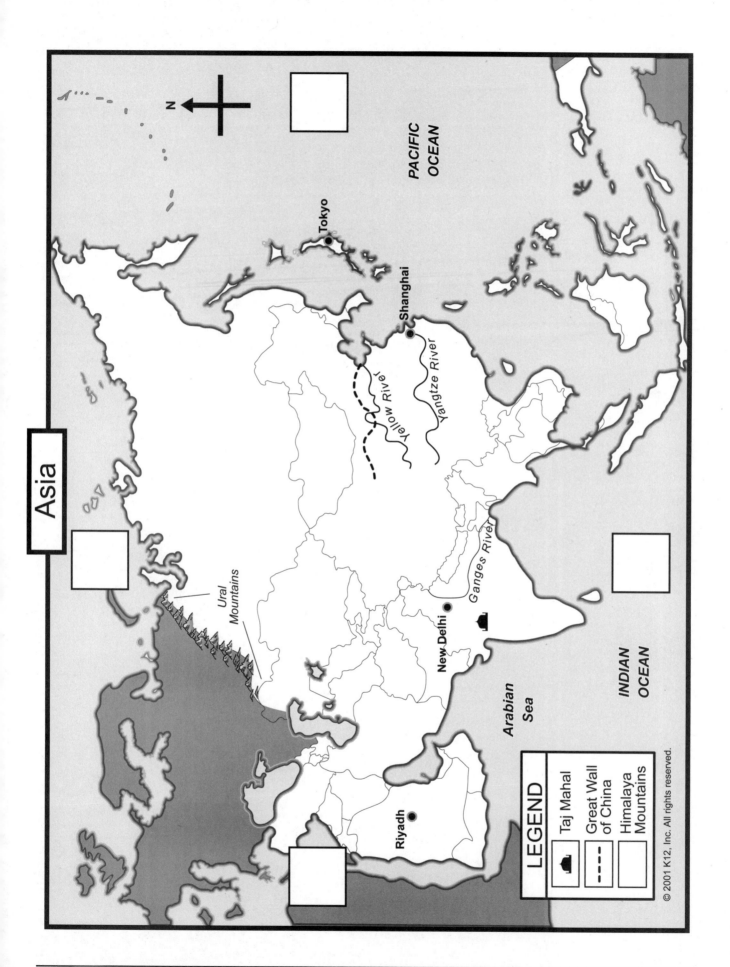

Asia

PACIFIC OCEAN

Tokyo

Shanghai

Yellow River

Yangtze River

Ganges River

Ural Mountains

New Delhi

Arabian Sea

INDIAN OCEAN

Riyadh

N

LEGEND

Taj Mahal

Great Wall of China

Himalaya Mountains

Student Guide
Lesson 1: Life in the Sahara

Travel to a large continent of deserts, rain forests, and grasslands, with amazingly varied animal life. Learn about the Sahara, the Kalahari Desert, the savanna, the Congo River, and the people who make their homes there.

Lesson Objectives

- Know that a desert is a dry area, usually covered with sand.
- Know that the Sahara is a large desert in Africa.
- Locate Africa on a globe.

PREPARE

Approximate lesson time is 45 minutes.

Advance Preparation

- In this lesson you will prepare salt dough. If you don't have the items already, please gather flour, salt, food coloring (blue, yellow, green, red), vegetable oil, cereal, and sandwich bags.

Materials

For the Student

- map of Africa
- suitcase cover

folder, manila

globe, inflatable

crayons, 16 or more

stapler

- People of the Sahara Coloring Sheet

bowl, large

Keywords and Pronunciation

eucalyp : A dry area, usually covered with sand.

lake : A large body of water, usually fresh, surrounded by land.

river : A long, flowing stream of fresh water.

sand dunes : Hills of sand created by winds.

turban : A long scarf wrapped around the head.

LEARN
Activity 1: Visit Africa *(Online)*

Activity 2: Ali of the Sahara *(Online)*

Activity 3: People of the Sahara *(Online)*

Activity 4: Make Dough for a Relief Map *(Online)*

ASSESS
Lesson Assessment: Life in the Sahara (*Online*)
You will complete an offline assessment covering the main objectives of this lesson. Your learning coach will score this assessment.

LEARN
Activity 5. Optional: Make a Sandpaper Picture *(Online)*

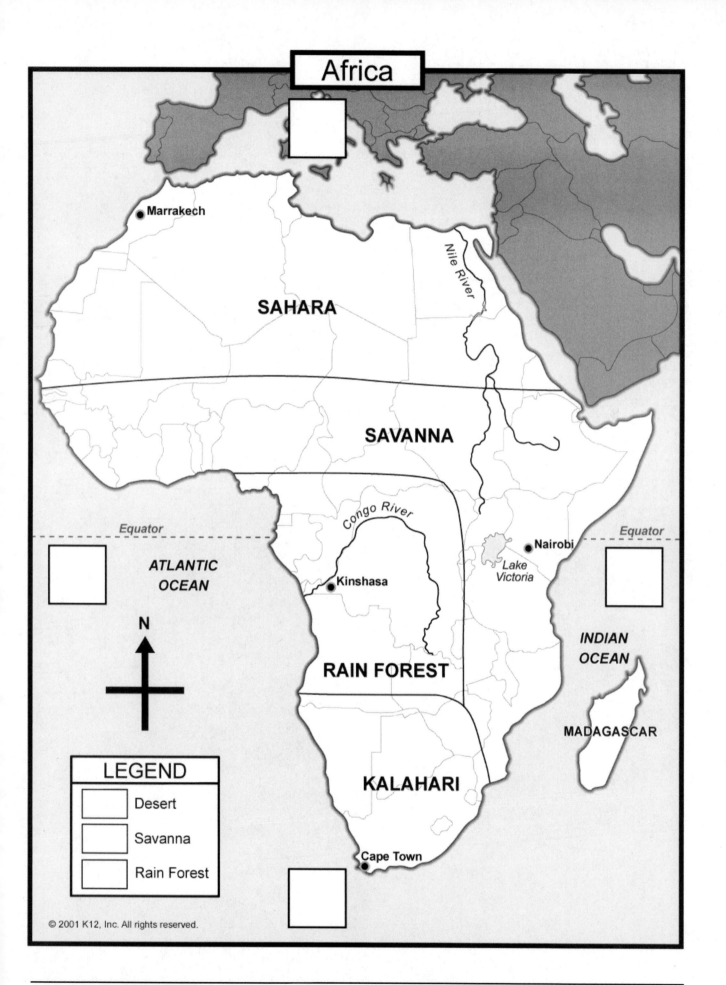

Africa

Marrakech

SAHARA

Nile River

SAVANNA

Equator

Congo River

ATLANTIC
OCEAN

Kinshasa

Nairobi

Lake
Victoria

Equator

N

RAIN FOREST

INDIAN
OCEAN

MADAGASCAR

KALAHARI

LEGEND

Desert

Savanna

Rain Forest

Cape Town

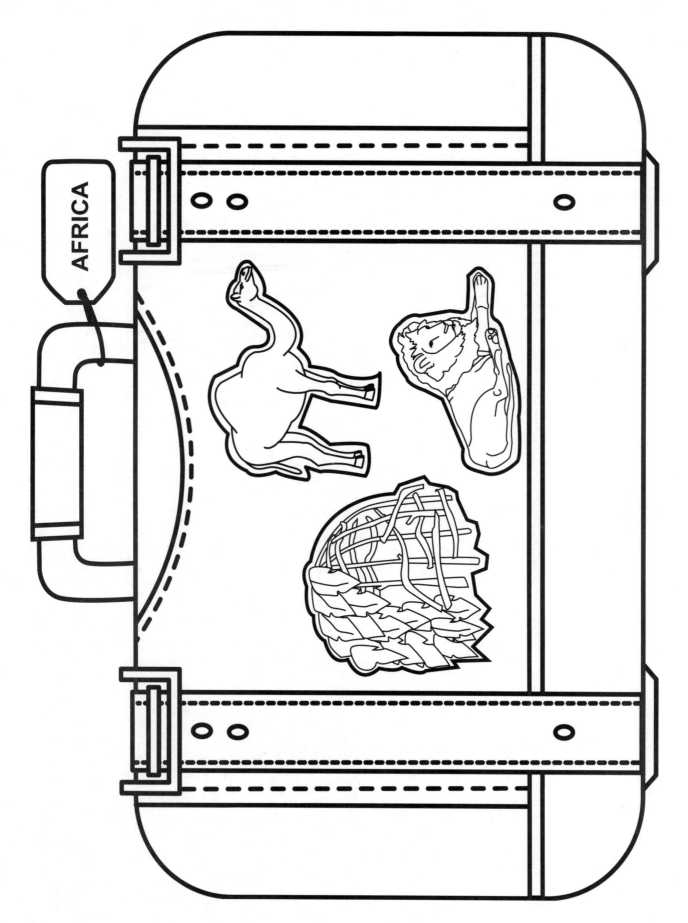

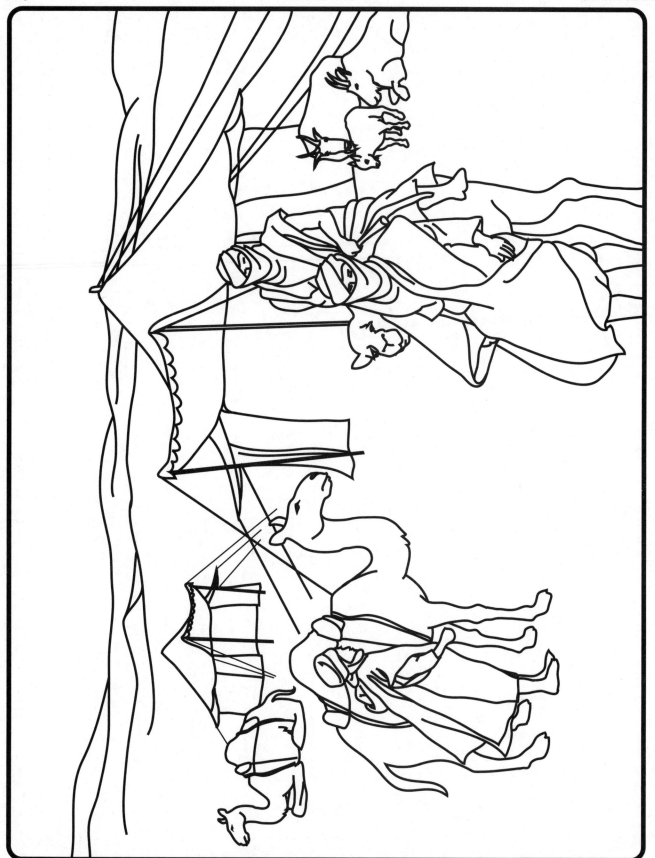

Lesson Assessment

Life in the Sahara

1. To answer this question, please use your globe of Earth. Where is the continent of Africa?

2. What is the name of the desert that Ali lives in?

3. What continent is the Sahara Desert on?

4. What is a desert?

Student Guide
Lesson 2. Optional: Southern Africa and the Kalahari Desert

Lesson Objectives

- Locate the Sahara on a map of Africa.
- Locate the Kalahari on a map of Africa.
- Describe an oasis as a place in the desert where things can grow because there is water.

PREPARE

Approximate lesson time is 45 minutes.

Advance Preparation

- For the activities in this lesson, you will need 3 cups of sand, blue plastic wrap, and an old, dry sponge.

Materials

For the Student

    🖥 map of Africa

    cardboard, boxes

    plastic wrap

    tape, clear

    crayons, 16 or more

    pan, baking

    salt

    sand, dry

    sponges

    water

    🖥 People of the Kalahari coloring sheet

Optional

    paints, tempera

    rock, smooth large

Keywords and Pronunciation

Kalahari (kah-lah-HAHR-ee)

Kede (KAY-day)

oasis (oh-AY-sis) : A place in the desert where things can grow because there is water.

salt pan : A shallow indentation in the earth filled with salt instead of water.

LEARN
Activity 1. Optional: Optional Lesson Instructions *(Online)*

This lesson is OPTIONAL. It is provided for students who seek enrichment or extra practice. You may skip this lesson.

If you choose to skip this lesson, then go to the Plan or Lesson Lists page and mark this lesson "Skipped" in order to proceed to the next lesson in the course.

Activity 2. Optional: Map of Africa *(Online)*

Activity 3. Optional: The Kalahari Desert *(Online)*

Activity 4. Optional: Construct the Kalahari *(Online)*

Activity 5. Optional: Kede of the Kalahari *(Online)*

Activity 6. Optional: Buried Water *(Online)*

Activity 7. Optional: The People of the Kalahari *(Online)*

Activity 8. Optional: Rock Art *(Online)*

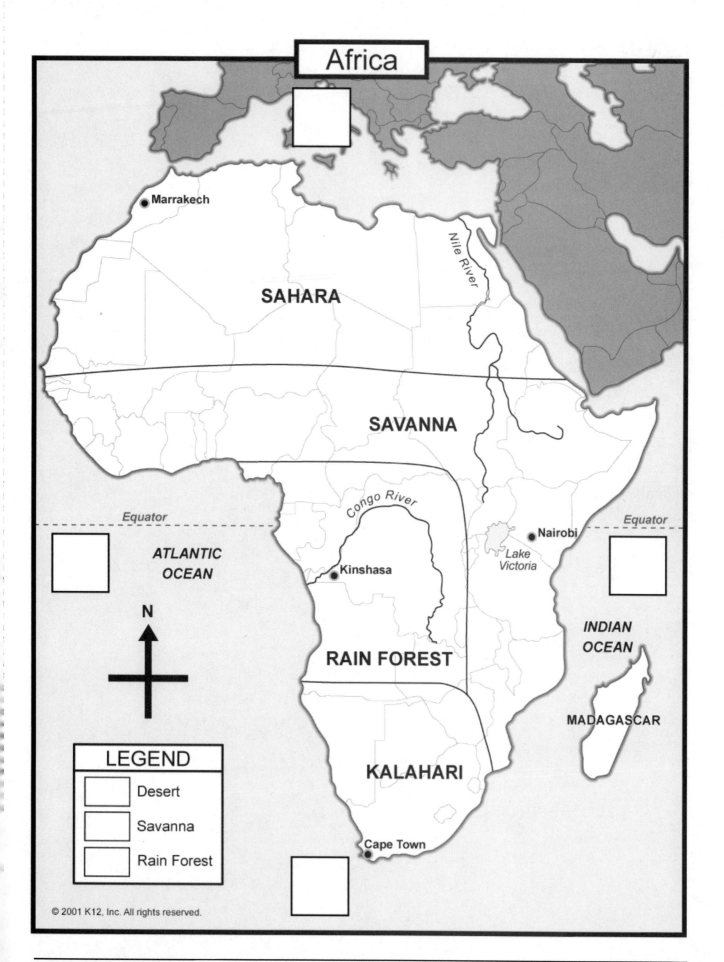

Africa

SAHARA

Nile River

SAVANNA

Marrakech

Congo River

Equator

ATLANTIC
OCEAN

Nairobi

Lake
Victoria

Equator

Kinshasa

N

INDIAN
OCEAN

RAIN FOREST

MADAGASCAR

KALAHARI

LEGEND

	Desert
	Savanna
	Rain Forest

Cape Town

Student Guide
Lesson 3: The African Savanna

From the desert, travel to a very different region, the savanna, home to some of Africa's most beautiful and fascinating animals, as well as the continent's largest lake.

Lesson Objectives

- Recognize a savanna as grassland.
- Associate the African savanna with animal life such as lions, zebras, and giraffes.

PREPARE

Approximate lesson time is 45 minutes.

Materials

For the Student

 🖥 map of Africa

 cardboard, boxes

 plastic wrap

 tape, clear

 crayons, 16 or more

 Bringing the Rain to Kapiti Plain by Verna Aardema (ISBN 0140546162)

 🖥 Animal Facts sheet

 🖥 Concentration Card sheet

 paper, colored construction, 12"x12" (2)

 Elmer's Glue-All

 scissors, round-end safety

Optional

 🖥 Masai People coloring sheet

 Rabbit Makes a Monkey of Lion: A Swahili Tale by Verna Aardema

 The Lonely Lioness and the Ostrich Chicks: A Masai Tale by Verna Aardema

 Who's in Rabbit's House: A Masai Tale by Verna Aardema

Keywords and Pronunciation

Masai (mah-SIY)

savanna : Grassland, or an open area of land covered with grass and occasional trees.

LEARN
Activity 1: Map of Africa *(Online)*

Activity 2: The Savanna *(Online)*

Activity 3: Kapiti Plain *(Online)*

Activity 4: African Concentration *(Online)*

Activity 5. Optional: The Masai of East Africa *(Online)*

ASSESS
Lesson Assessment: The African Savanna (*Online*)
You will complete an offline assessment covering the main objectives of this lesson. Your learning coach will score this assessment.

LEARN
Activity 6. Optional: Read one of the following *(Online)*

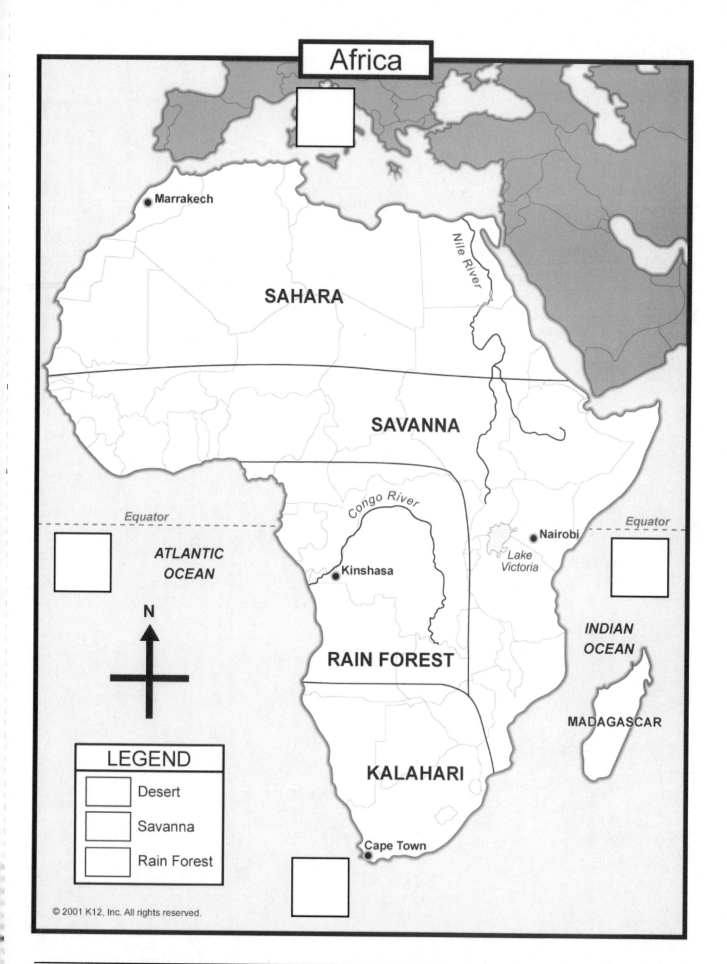

Africa

Marrakech

SAHARA

Nile River

SAVANNA

Congo River

Equator

ATLANTIC
OCEAN

Kinshasa

Nairobi

Lake
Victoria

Equator

INDIAN
OCEAN

N

RAIN FOREST

MADAGASCAR

KALAHARI

LEGEND

Desert

Savanna

Rain Forest

Cape Town

Animal Facts

Sable antelope have long horns with a slight curve. They are glossy black, except for the white hair on their face, ears, and belly. They get all the water they need by munching on the grasses of the savanna.

Cape buffalo are easy to recognize by their huge, upward-swerving horns. They travel in herds to protect themselves from lions. They live near watering holes on the savanna.

Cheetahs are the fastest animals on land. Their long tails help them balance when they make high-speed turns. A cheetah doesn't roar like a lion, but purrs like a cat.

Elephants are the largest animals in Africa. An elephant uses the tip of its trunk the same way you use your fingers. Elephants flap their ears like a fan to stay cool.

Giraffes have long necks, which are a great help for eating the leaves of trees. In fact, giraffes spend more than half of each day eating, even though they can go without water for weeks at a time.

Spotted hyenas look like scruffy dogs. They are good hunters and eat the bones, hair, and hooves of any animals they catch.

Lions are known as the king of animals. Lions are actually wild cats. The male has a bushy mane. Its African name is Simba.

Patas monkeys eat leaves, flowers, and insects on the savanna. Cheetahs and lions hunt Patas monkeys, so they never stray very far from trees where they can hide. Patas monkeys have reddish fur and gray chin whiskers.

Ostriches are the largest birds. (They might remind you of the Australian emu.) They have black feathers with white plumes on their tails and wings. Ostriches travel in herds with a leader who decides where they will eat.

African rock pythons come in many different colors. Some are brown. Some are black and yellow. Some are green. But no matter what their color, they all are longer than six feet—and they all swallow their food.

Rhinoceroses are thick-skinned animals with one or two horns on their snout. They have really bad eyesight, but a great sense of smell.

Zebras look like horses, except that they are covered with black and white stripes. Zebras bathe practically every day—in dust! They live in family units of 20 or so animals.

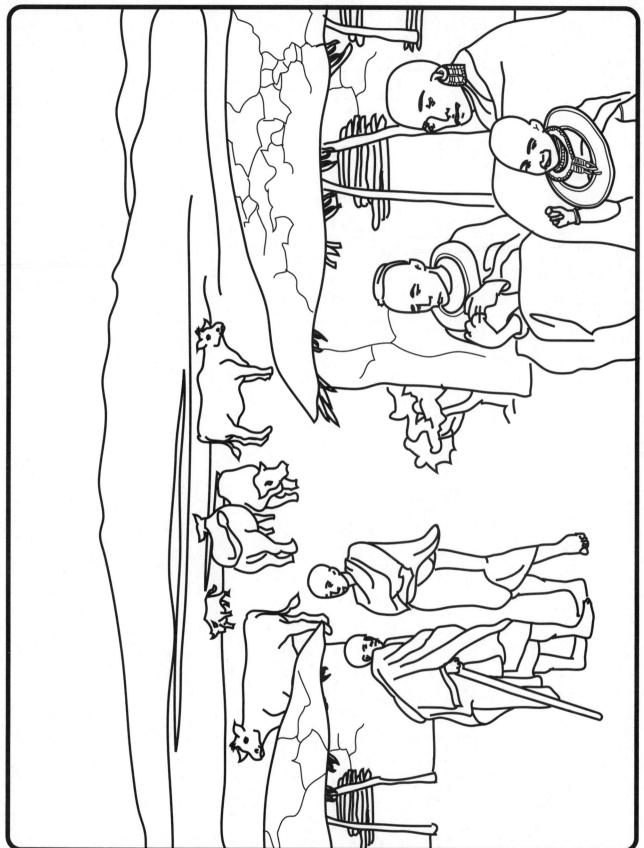

Lesson Assessment

The African Savanna

1. What will you see in the savanna instead of sand and rocks?

2. What are some of the animals you would see in the savanna?

Student Guide
Lesson 4: Central Africa and the Congo Rain Forest

From the deserts and savanna of Africa, we move on to explore a very different region—the rain forest of the Congo.

Lesson Objectives

- Identify two characteristics of a rain forest.
- Locate the Congo River on a map of Africa.
- Locate the Sahara on a map of Africa.
- Locate the savanna on a map of Africa.

PREPARE

Approximate lesson time is 45 minutes.

Materials

For the Student

    🖾 map of Africa

    globe, inflatable

    crayons, 16 or more

    🖾 Pygmies of the Congo coloring sheet

Optional

    bags, brown paper grocery

    paints, watercolor, 8 colors or more

    scissors, round-end safety

    string

    beans, dried

    containers, oatmeal

    glue sticks

    paper, colored construction, 12"x12"

    fabric

    markers, colored, 8 or more

    rubber bands

    tape, clear

    gravel

    plants, small green (2)

    soil, potting

    household items - Charcoal

    jar, large glass

    plastic wrap

Keywords and Pronunciation

Mbuti (em-BOO-tee)

pygmies (PIG-mees)

tropical rain forest : A thick forest located near the equator where it rains much of the time.

LEARN
Activity 1: Thinking About Africa (Online)

Activity 2: A River and a Rain Forest (Online)

Activity 3: Kaboto Goes Hunting (Online)

Activity 4: The Pygmies of the Congo Rain Forest (Online)

Activity 5. Optional: Make a Loincloth (Online)

Activity 6. Optional: A Tribal Drum (Online)

ASSESS

Lesson Assessment: Central Africa and the Congo Rain Forest (Online)

You will complete an offline assessment covering the main objectives of this lesson. Your learning coach will score this assessment.

LEARN
Activity 7. Optional: Rain Forest in a Jar (Online)

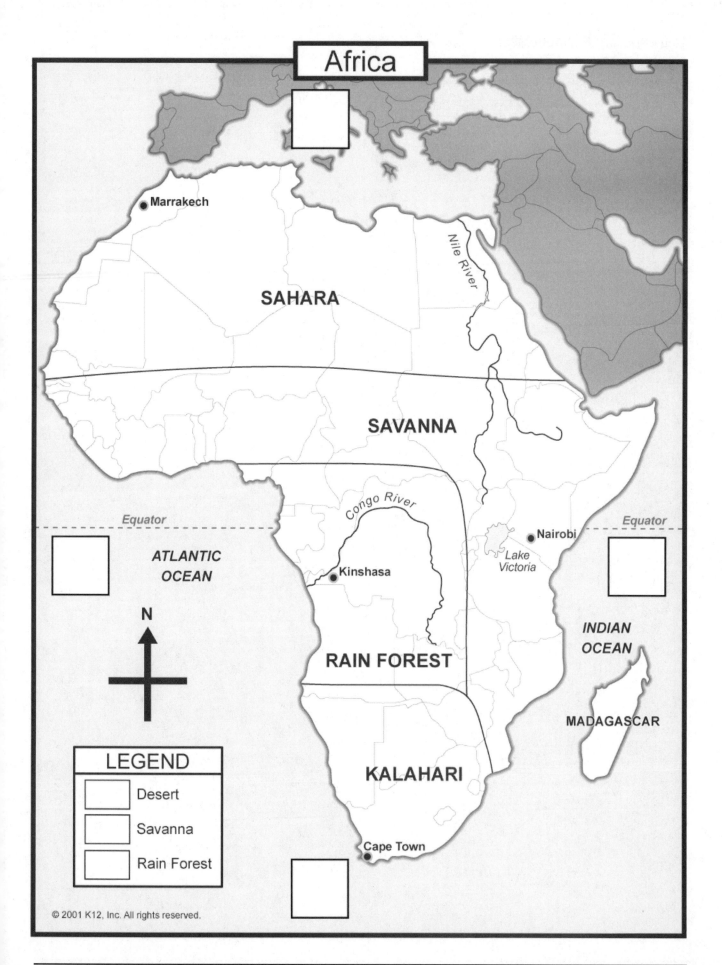

Africa

Marrakech

SAHARA

Nile River

SAVANNA

Congo River

Equator

ATLANTIC
OCEAN

Nairobi

Lake
Victoria

Equator

INDIAN
OCEAN

Kinshasa

N

RAIN FOREST

MADAGASCAR

KALAHARI

LEGEND

Desert

Savanna

Rain Forest

Cape Town

225

Name _____   Date _____

Lesson Assessment

Central Africa and the Congo Rain Forest

1. To answer this question, please use your map of Africa.
   Where is the Sahara located?

2. To answer this question, please use your map of Africa.
   Where is the savanna located?

3. To answer this question, please use your map of Africa.
   Where is the Congo River located?

4. Name at least two characteristics of the rain forest.

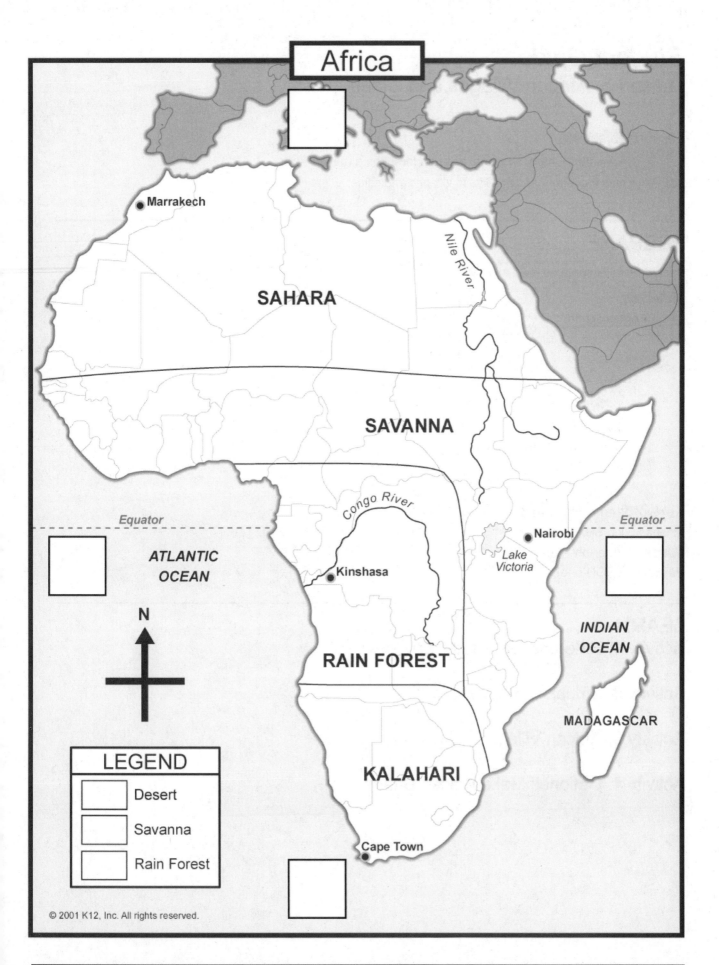

Africa

SAHARA

Nile River

SAVANNA

Marrakech

Congo River

Equator

ATLANTIC OCEAN

Kinshasa

Nairobi

Lake Victoria

Equator

INDIAN OCEAN

N

RAIN FOREST

MADAGASCAR

KALAHARI

LEGEND

	Desert
	Savanna
	Rain Forest

Cape Town

Student Guide
Lesson 5: African Villages and Cities

Lesson Objectives

- Locate the Sahara, savanna, and rain forest on a map of Africa.
- Know that many Africans live in villages and cities.

PREPARE

Approximate lesson time is 45 minutes.

Materials

For the Student

- 🖳 map of Africa

Optional

> flour
>
> cookie sheet
>
> pipe cleaners
>
> scissors, round-end safety
>
> string
>
> toothpicks

Keywords and Pronunciation

Kinshasa (kin-SHAH-suh)

Marrakech (mer-uh-KESH)

Nairobi (niy-ROH-bee)

LEARN
Activity 1: Hide-and-Seek in Africa *(Online)*

Activity 2: African Cities *(Online)*

Activity 3: African Villages *(Online)*

Activity 4. Optional: Make African Beads *(Online)*

ASSESS
Lesson Assessment: African Villages and Cities (*Online*)

You will complete an offline assessment covering the main objectives of this lesson. Your learning coach will score this assessment.

LEARN
Activity 5. Optional: Communicating in Africa (*Online*)

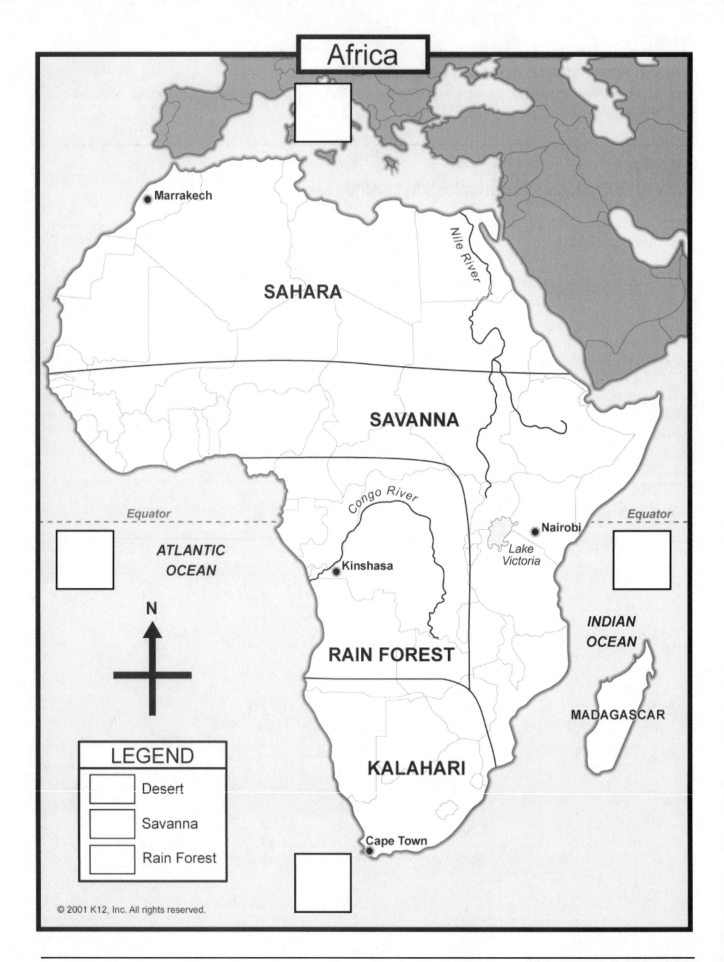

Africa

Marrakech

SAHARA

Nile River

SAVANNA

Congo River

Equator

ATLANTIC
OCEAN

RAIN FOREST

Kinshasa

Lake
Victoria

Nairobi

Equator

INDIAN
OCEAN

N

MADAGASCAR

KALAHARI

LEGEND

Desert

Savanna

Rain Forest

Cape Town

Lesson Assessment

African Villages and Cities

1. To answer this question, please use your map of Africa.
    Where are the Sahara, the savanna, and the rain forest located?

2. Where do many Africans live?

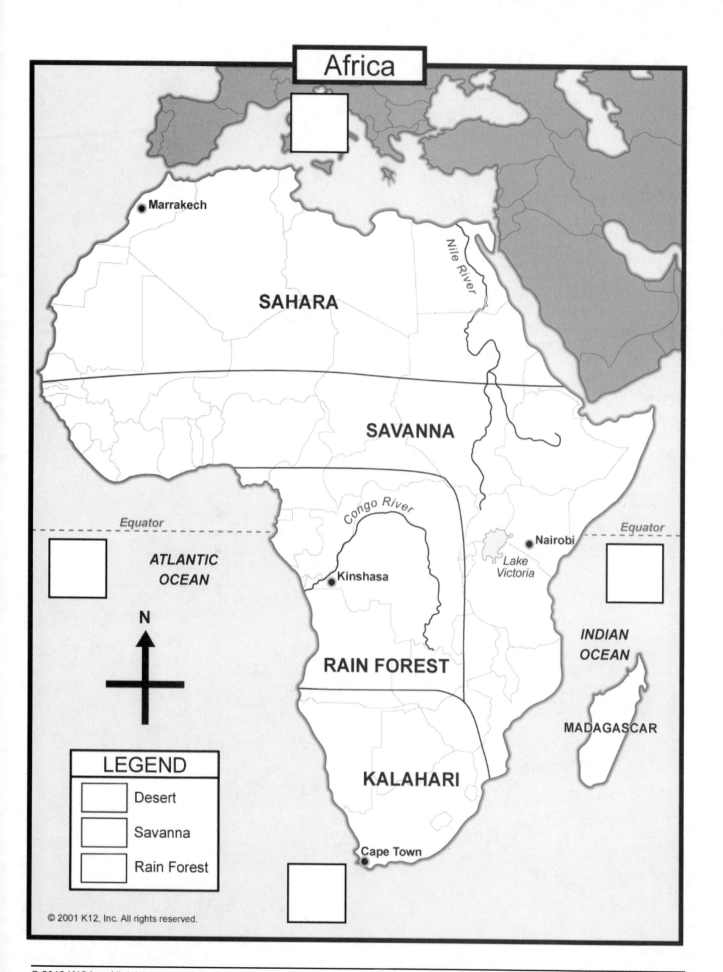

Africa

Marrakech

SAHARA

Nile River

SAVANNA

Congo River

Equator

ATLANTIC
OCEAN

Kinshasa

Lake
Victoria

Nairobi

Equator

INDIAN
OCEAN

N

RAIN FOREST

MADAGASCAR

LEGEND

Desert

Savanna

Rain Forest

KALAHARI

Cape Town

Student Guide
Lesson 1: The Amazon Rain Forest

Explore South America, from the Andes Mountains to the vast regions of the Amazon River. South America is home to the worlds largest rain forest and some of the world's most amazing animals. Visit Brazil, and then journey to the grasslands of the pampas.

The tropical rain forests of the world lie near the equator. The biggest and most diverse is the Amazon rain forest of South America. In this lesson, your student will visit the forest and meet some of the amazing animals.

Lesson Objectives

- Locate South America on a globe.
- Locate the Amazon River and Amazon rain forest on a map of South America.
- Know that creatures live in the layers of the Amazon rain forest.

PREPARE

Approximate lesson time is 45 minutes.

Materials

For the Student

- map of South America
- South America suitcase cover
- crayons, 16 or more
- file folder
- globe, inflatable
- Mr. Traveler Figurine
- Elmer's Glue-All
- stapler
- The Great Kapok Tree by Lynne Cherry (ISBN 152026142)
- Kapok Tree coloring sheet
- Rain Forest Animals cutout sheet
- Where Do They Live definition sheet
- scissors, round-end safety

Optional

- Blue Morpho Butterfly pattern
- glue sticks
- paper, colored construction, 12"x12" (2)
- markers, colored, 8 or more
- pipe cleaners (2)
- tape, clear

Keywords and Pronunciation
morpho (MOR-foh)

LEARN
Activity 1: Traveling to South America *(Online)*

Activity 2: Animals of the Amazon Rain Forest *(Online)*

Activity 3: Read Aloud *(Online)*

Activity 4: Where Do They Live? *(Online)*

Activity 5. Optional: Make a Blue Morpho *(Online)*

ASSESS
Lesson Assessment: The Amazon Rain Forest (*Online*)
You will complete an offline assessment covering the main objectives of this lesson. Your learning coach will score this assessment.

South America

ATLANTIC
OCEAN

Equator

Amazon River

BRAZIL

Andes

Mountains

Rio de Janeiro •

PACIFIC
OCEAN

ATLANTIC
OCEAN

N

LEGEND

Amazon Rain Forest

Pampas

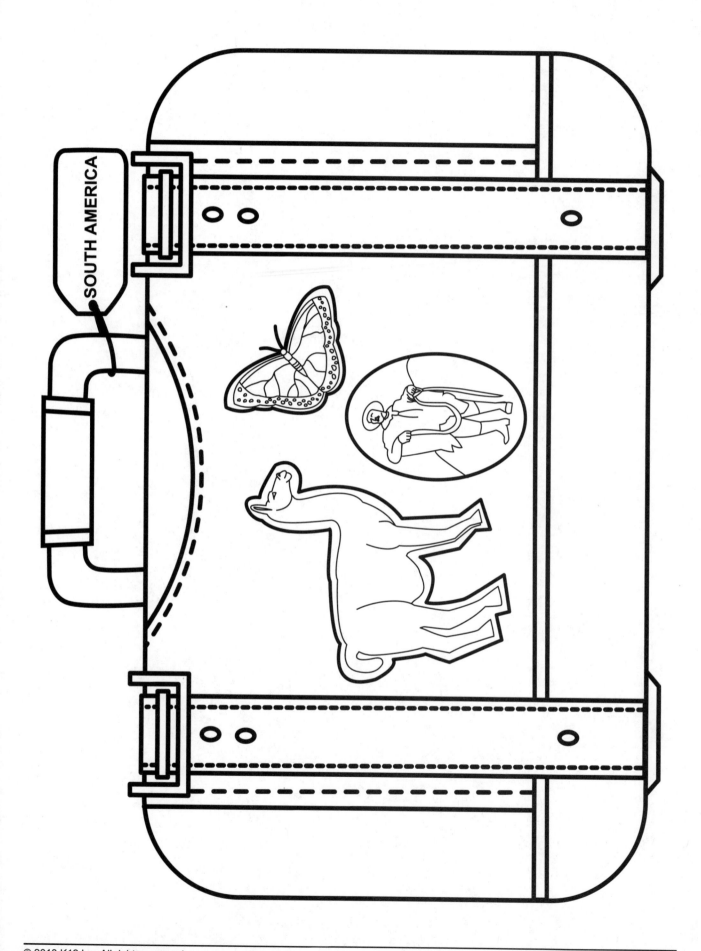

SOUTH AMERICA

Where Do They Live Definition Sheet

I am an **emerald tree boa**. I slither through the branches looking for birds to eat. It's hard to see me because I blend in with the leaves. What layer do I live in? (canopy)

I am a **squirrel monkey**. I purr, bark, and scream as I scamper from one tree to another. When I'm not munching on bugs and bananas, I like to hang from my tail from high branches. What layer do I live in? (canopy)

I am a **toucan**. I eat the berries I find growing high in the trees. I'll snatch one, flip it into the air, and catch it in my mouth. What layer do I live in? (canopy)

I am a **blue morpho butterfly**. My wings are bright blue on top, but black underneath. I live off the juices I find in flowers. What layer do I live in? (understory)

I am a **jaguar**. I sleep in low tree branches but hunt animals on the ground. I am also a good swimmer. What layer do I live in? (understory)

I am a **tree porcupine**. Look up! You may see me hanging upside down by my tail on low branches. I look a bit like an echidna. I eat fruits and nuts. What layer do I live in? (the canopy)

I am a **giant anteater**. I crawl around on my knuckles looking for anthills. When I find one, I tear it open with my sharp claws and suck out all the ants with my long sticky tongue. What layer do I live in? (understory)

I am a **three-toed sloth**, the slowest moving animal in the jungle. I move so slowly that my fur turns green with mold. I eat berries and leaves while I hang from the tree branches. What layer do I live in? (canopy)

I am a **tapir**, the largest animal in the rain forest. I can't fly or climb trees, but I can run really fast. I eat leaves and grasses near the river, where I love to swim. What layer do I live in? (understory)

Canopy

Understory

cut

Lesson Assessment

The Amazon Rain Forest

1. To answer this question, please use your globe.
   Where is South America located?

2. To answer this question, please use your map of South America.
   Where are the Amazon River and the Amazon rain forest located?

3. Where do different creatures live in the Amazon rain forest?

South America

ATLANTIC OCEAN

Equator   Equator

Amazon River

BRAZIL

Andes

Mountains

PACIFIC OCEAN

Rio de Janeiro •

ATLANTIC OCEAN

N

LEGEND

Amazon Rain Forest

Pampas

© 2001 K12, Inc. All rights reserved.

Student Guide
Lesson 2: It Comes from Brazil

Brazil, the biggest country in South America, is a country rich in natural resources. In this lesson, your student will learn that certain items around the house or available at a local store might have come from Brazil.

Lesson Objectives
- Locate Brazil on a map of South America.
- Know that many things we use come from Brazil.

PREPARE

Approximate lesson time is 45 minutes.

Materials
For the Student

    📖 map of South America

    globe, inflatable

    Mr. Traveler Figurine

    crayons, 16 or more

    magazines

    sugar

    fruits

    index cards, 4" x 6"

    rubber bands

    📖 It comes from Brazil activity sheet

    pencils, no. 2

Keywords and Pronunciation
Rio de Janeiro (REE-oh day zhuh-NER-oh)

LEARN
Activity 1: Traveling to Brazil (Online)

Activity 2: Rio de Janeiro (Online)

Activity 3: Brazil's Natural Resources *(Online)*

Activity 4: It Comes from Brazil *(Online)*

ASSESS

Lesson Assessment: It Comes from Brazil (*Online*)

You will complete an offline assessment covering the main objectives of this lesson. Your learning coach will score this assessment.

South America

ATLANTIC
OCEAN

Equator

Amazon River

Equator

BRAZIL

Andes

Mountains

Rio de Janeiro •

PACIFIC
OCEAN

ATLANTIC
OCEAN

N

LEGEND

Amazon Rain Forest

Pampas

1

Oranges

It Comes from Brazil

4

Rubber

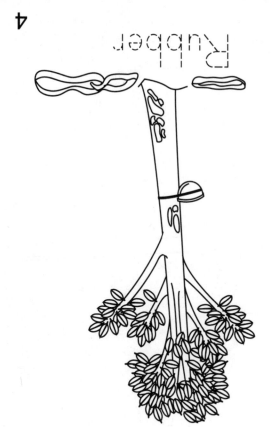

Coffee

2

Sugar

3

Name _____   Date _____

Lesson Assessment

It Comes From Brazil

1. To answer this question, please use your map of South America.
   Where is the country of Brazil?

2. Name two natural resources of Brazil.

South America

ATLANTIC OCEAN

Equator

Amazon River

Equator

BRAZIL

Andes

Mountains

Rio de Janeiro •

PACIFIC OCEAN

ATLANTIC OCEAN

N

LEGEND

Amazon Rain Forest

Pampas

History
                                 Samba in South America
                                     It Comes from Brazil

1

Oranges

4

Rubber

It Comes from Brazil

Coffee

2

Sugar

3

Student Guide
Lesson 3: High in the Andes

High on the west coast of South America rise the rugged Andes Mountains. Far removed from modern society, the people of the Andes rely on their animals and each other to survive.

Lesson Objectives

- Describe life in the Andes Mountains.
- Locate the Andes Mountains on a map of South America.

PREPARE

Approximate lesson time is 45 minutes.

Materials

For the Student

    The Great Kapok Tree by Lynne Cherry (ISBN 152026142)

    Mr. Traveler Figurine

    🖥 map of South America

    crayons, 16 or more

Optional

    🖥 Mountain Life activity sheet

    🖥 Llama and Alpacas activity sheet

    cotton balls

    glue sticks

    dirt

    knife, butter

    cookie sheet

Keywords and Pronunciation

Andes (AN-deez)

Quechua (KECH-wuh) : a group of Native Americans in Peru who speak an ancient Inca language

Quechua (KECH-wuh)

Saman (SAW-mawn)

terracing : Cutting steps into a mountainside in order to grow crops on level land.

LEARN
Activity 1: Animals and Resources *(Online)*

Activity 2: **More About South America** (Online)

Activity 3: **A Typical Day for Saman** (Online)

Activity 4. Optional: **Quechua Life in the Andes** (Online)

Activity 5. Optional: **Llamas and Alpacas** (Online)

ASSESS

Lesson Assessment: High in the Andes (*Online*)

You will complete an offline assessment covering the main objectives of this lesson. Your learning coach will score this assessment.

LEARN

Activity 6. Optional: Make a Terrace (Online)

South America

ATLANTIC OCEAN

Equator

Amazon River

Equator

BRAZIL

Andes

Mountains

Rio de Janeiro •

ATLANTIC OCEAN

PACIFIC OCEAN

N

LEGEND

Amazon Rain Forest

Pampas

1.

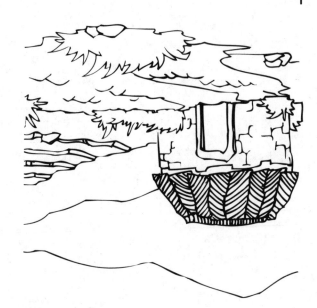

Quechua Life in the Andes

4.

2.

3.

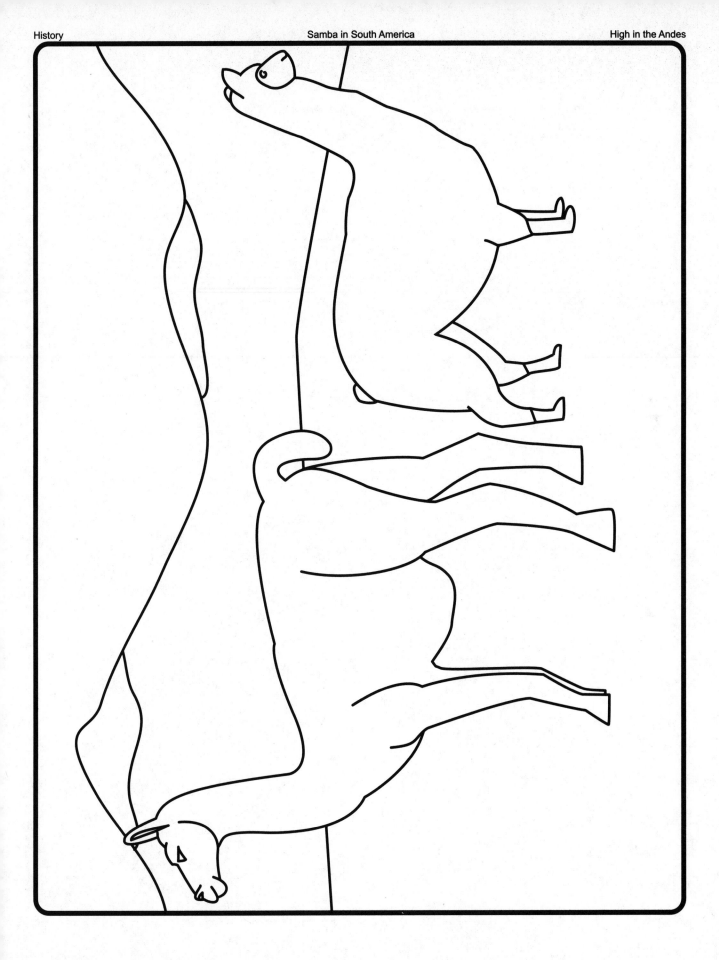

Lesson Assessment

High in the Andes

1. To answer this question, please use your map of South America.
   Where are the Andes Mountains?

2. What is life like in the Andes Mountains?

South America

ATLANTIC
OCEAN

Equator

Amazon River

Equator

BRAZIL

Andes

Mountains

Rio de Janeiro

PACIFIC
OCEAN

N

ATLANTIC
OCEAN

LEGEND

Amazon Rain Forest

Pampas

Student Guide
Lesson 4: On the Pampas

The grasslands of South America are known as the pampas. In this lesson, meet a boy who wants to grow up to be just like [NGT]his father-a hard-working gaucho on the pampas.

Lesson Objectives

- Locate the pampas on a map of South America.
- Identify the pampas as South American grasslands.
- Know that a gaucho is a South American cowboy.

PREPARE

Approximate lesson time is 45 minutes.

Materials

For the Student

    📖 map of South America

    crayons, 16 or more

    📖 Paolo activity sheet

Optional

    📖 Lasso Action flip book

    scissors, round-end safety

    stapler

    The Magic Bean Tree: A Legend from Argentina by Nancy Van Laan

    paper, drawing

Keywords and Pronunciation

Centella (sen-TAY-juh)

gaucho : A South American cowboy.

gauchos (GOW-chohs)

mate (MAH-tay)

Melazas (may-LAH-szahs)

pampas (PAHM-puhz) : The grasslands of South America.

Paolo (PAH-oh-loh)

siesta (see-ES-tuh) : An afternoon nap.

LEARN
Activity 1: Reviewing South America *(Online)*

Activity 2: Read Aloud *(Online)*

Activity 3: Make Paolo a Gaucho *(Online)*

Activity 4: Beat the Clock: Where in the World? *(Online)*

Activity 5. Optional: Lasso Action Flip Book *(Online)*

ASSESS

Lesson Assessment: On the Pampas (*Online*)

You will complete an offline assessment covering the main objectives of this lesson. Your learning coach will score this assessment.

LEARN
Activity 6. Optional: Suggested Reading *(Online)*

South America

ATLANTIC OCEAN

Equator

Equator

Amazon River

BRAZIL

Andes

Mountains

Rio de Janeiro

PACIFIC OCEAN

ATLANTIC OCEAN

N

LEGEND

Amazon Rain Forest

Pampas

✂ cut

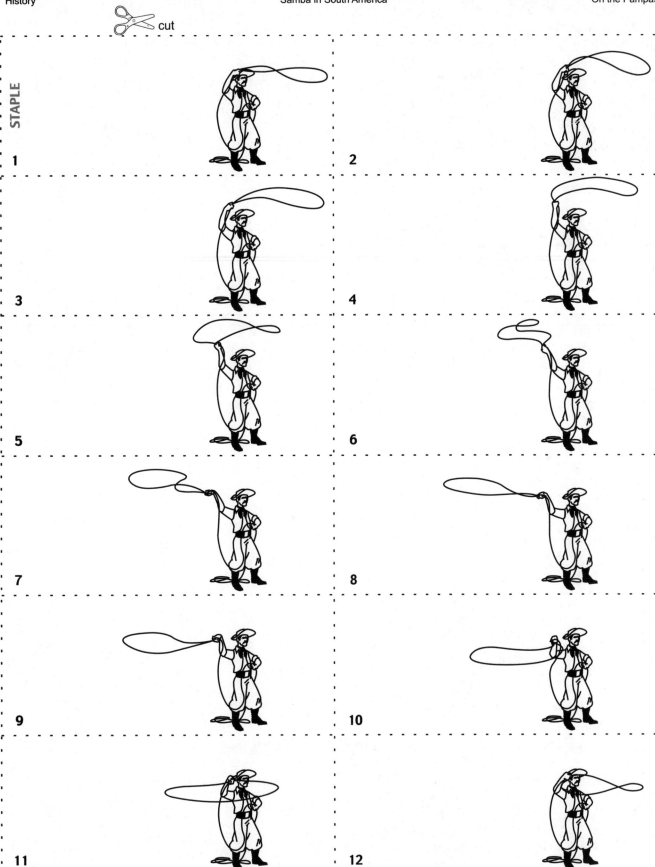

Lesson Assessment

On the Pampas

1. To answer this question, please use your map of South America. Where are the pampas located?

2. What are the South American grasslands called?

3. What is a gaucho?

South America

ATLANTIC
OCEAN

Equator   Equator

Amazon River

BRAZIL

Andes

Mountains

Rio de Janeiro •

PACIFIC
OCEAN

ATLANTIC
OCEAN

N

LEGEND

Amazon Rain Forest

Pampas

287

Student Guide
Lesson 1: Land of Ice and Snow

Travel to the South Pole and visit Antarctica, a continent of snow, ice, and blizzards. Meet the hardy animals, including some remarkably rugged penguins, for whom this coldest of all continents is home.

Antarctica is a continent of ice, snow, and blizzards. No humans call Antarctica home, but there are several groups of animals that have adapted to life in the Antarctic climate.

Lesson Objectives

- Locate Antarctica on a globe.
- Locate the South Pole on the map of Antarctica.
- Understand that no humans call Antarctica home.

PREPARE

Approximate lesson time is 45 minutes.

Materials

For the Student
- 📖 Antarctica suitcase cover
- 📖 map of Antarctica
- folder, manila
- globe, inflatable
- Mr. Traveler Figurine
- paper, colored construction, 12"x12"
- crayons, 16 or more
- stapler
- tubs, margarine

Optional
- plastic sandwich bags, zipper-closed (3)
- solid shortening
- ice

Keywords and Pronunciation

glacier (GLAY-shur) : A huge, very slow-moving mass of ice that is formed on land from snow falling and building up over many years.

iceberg : A huge piece of ice floating in the water.

LEARN

Activity 1: Sing Along *(Online)*

Activity 2: The Coldest Continent *(Online)*

Activity 3: Make an Iceberg *(Online)*

Activity 4: Animals of Antarctica *(Online)*

Activity 5. Optional: Blubber Glove *(Online)*

ASSESS

Lesson Assessment: Land of Ice and Snow (*Online*)

You will complete an offline assessment covering the main objectives of this lesson. Your learning coach will score this assessment.

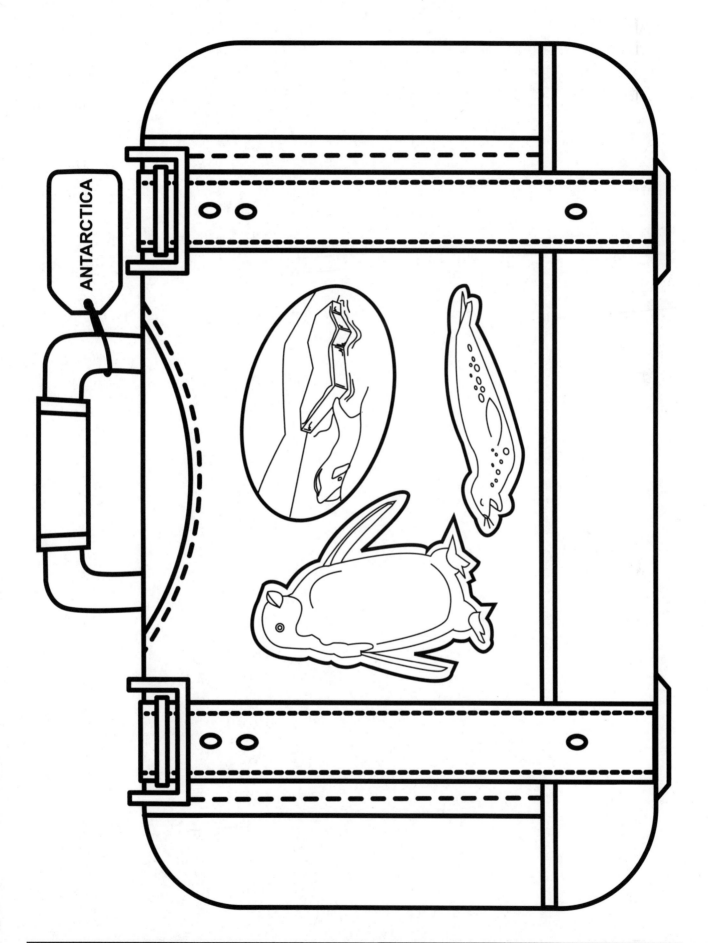

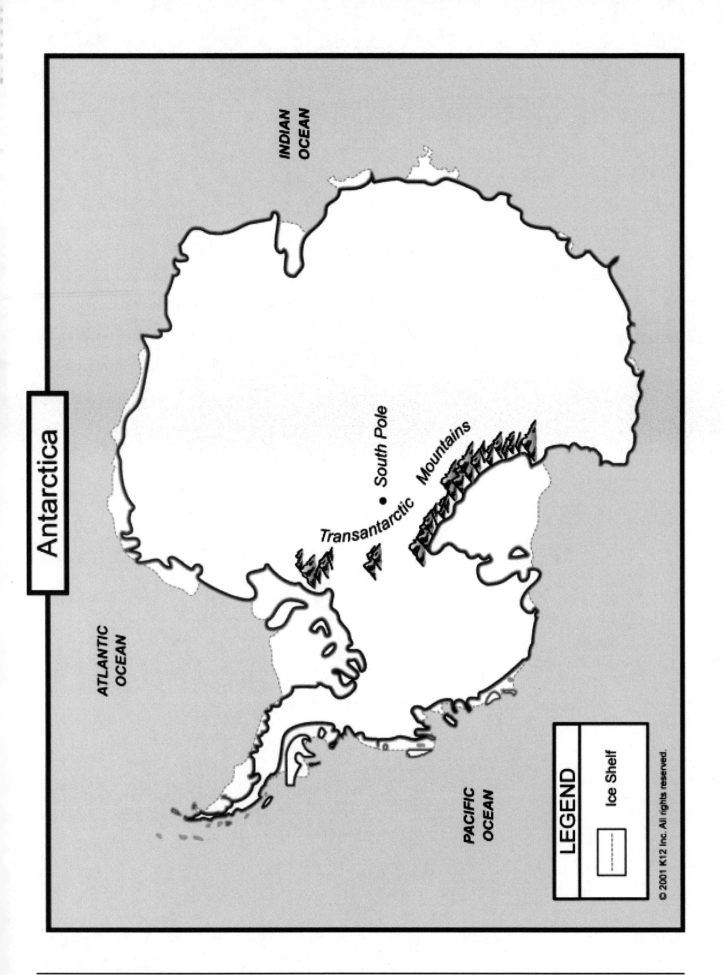

Antarctica

INDIAN OCEAN

South Pole

Transantarctic Mountains

ATLANTIC OCEAN

PACIFIC OCEAN

LEGEND

Ice Shelf

Name _____   Date _____

Lesson Assessment

Land of Ice and Snow

1. To answer this question, please use your globe.
   Where is Antarctica located?

2. To answer this question, please use your map of Antarctica.
   Where is the South Pole located?

3. Do any humans call Antarctica home?

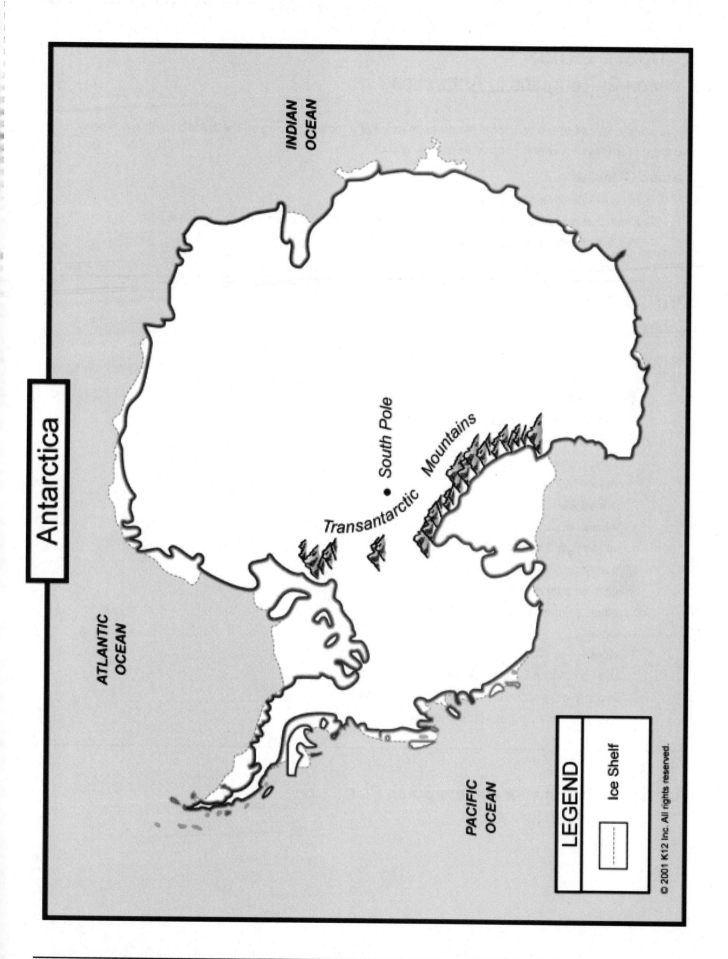

Antarctica

INDIAN OCEAN

ATLANTIC OCEAN

• South Pole

Transantarctic Mountains

PACIFIC OCEAN

LEGEND

Ice Shelf

Student Guide
Lesson 2: Penguins in Antarctica

While no people call Antarctica home, some animals have adapted to living on the coldest continent. Today we learn more about a very cool creature-the penguin.

Lesson Objectives

- Locate Antarctica on a globe.
- Know that places near the equator are usually warm and places near the poles are cold.
- Know that penguins live in Antarctica.

PREPARE

Approximate lesson time is 45 minutes.

Materials

For the Student

    globe, inflatable

    toys - small plastic boat

Optional

    🖳 Penguins in Antarctica

    crayons, 16 or more

    glue sticks

    pencils, no. 2

    scissors, round-end safety

    markers, colored, 8 or more

    glasses, drinking (2)

    paper, colored construction, 12"x12"

    spoon

    water

    Antarctic Antics by Judy Sierra

    Seven Weeks on an Iceberg by Keith R. Potter

    The Emperor's Egg by Martin Jenkins

LEARN
Activity 1: The Equator and the South Pole *(Online)*

Activity 2: Float Your Iceberg (Online)

Activity 3: A Penguin Family (Online)

Activity 4: Show You Know (Online)

Activity 5: Around the Globe (Online)

Activity 6. Optional: Penguin Project (Online)

Activity 7. Optional: Match the Sound (Online)

ASSESS

Lesson Assessment: Penguins in Antarctica (*Online*)

You will complete an offline assessment covering the main objectives of this lesson. Your learning coach will score this assessment.

LEARN

Activity 8. Optional: Reading About Penguins (Online)

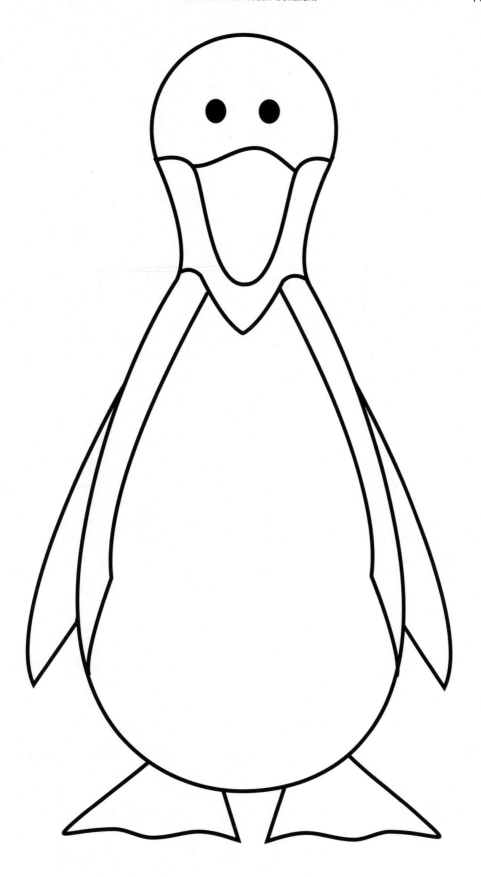

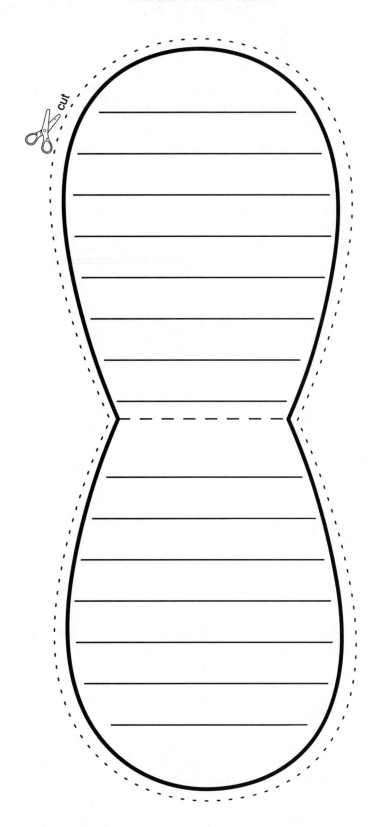

Name _____ Date _____

Lesson Assessment

Penguins in Antarctica

1. Are places near the equator warm?

2. Are places near the North or South Pole cold?

3. To answer this question, please use your globe.
   Where is the continent of Antarctica located?

4. What is the name of the continent near the South Pole where many penguins live?

Student Guide
Lesson 1: Oh, Canada!

Explore the North American continent and learn more about three great nations and the geographical wonders found there. Journey north for a tour of Canada, then south to Mexico for some fiesta fun. Conclude your tour in the U.S.A., where this land is your land.

In this visit to Canada, the second-largest country in the world, we'll see some of the wonders of the landscape and meet some of the people and animals that live in Canada.

Lesson Objectives

- Locate Canada on a map of North America.
- Locate North America on a globe.
- Identify the maple leaf as the symbol of Canada.

PREPARE

Approximate lesson time is 45 minutes.

Materials

For the Student

    🖥 map of North America

    🖥 suitcase cover

    folder, manila

    globe, inflatable

    crayons, 16 or more

    stapler

Optional

    🖥 Maple Leaf Pattern

    glue sticks

    paper, colored construction, 12"x12"

    pencils, no. 2

    ruler, standard 12"

    scissors, round-end safety

Keywords and Pronunciation

Inuit (IH-nou-wuht)

LEARN
Activity 1: Get Ready for North America *(Online)*

Activity 2: Welcome to Canada! *(Online)*

Activity 3: A Tour of Canada *(Online)*

Activity 4: The Inuit *(Online)*

Activity 5. Optional: Canada's Flag *(Online)*

ASSESS
Lesson Assessment: Oh, Canada! (*Online*)

You will complete an offline assessment covering the main objectives of this lesson. Your learning coach will score this assessment.

LEARN
Activity 6. Optional: Firsts from Canada *(Online)*

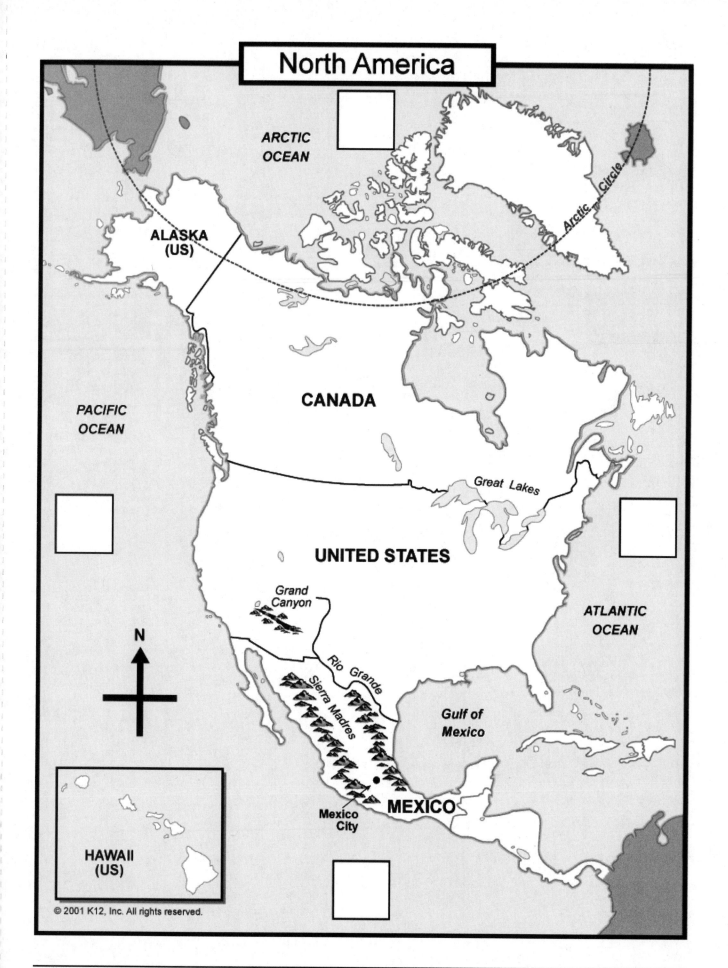

North America

ARCTIC OCEAN

ALASKA (US)

Arctic Circle

CANADA

PACIFIC OCEAN

Great Lakes

UNITED STATES

Grand Canyon

Rio Grande

ATLANTIC OCEAN

N

Sierra Madres

Gulf of Mexico

MEXICO

Mexico City

HAWAII (US)

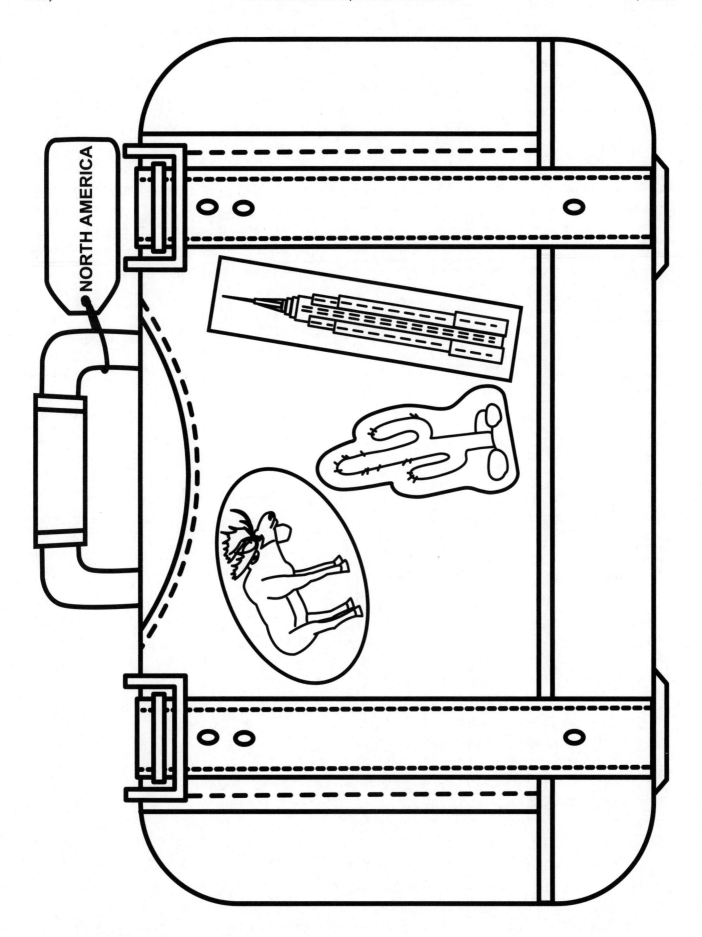

NORTH AMERICA

Maple Leaf

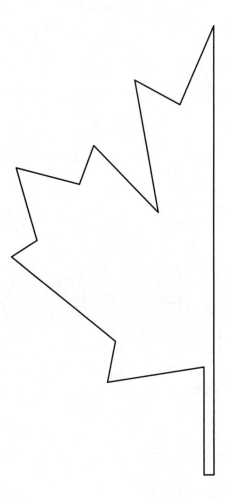

Lesson Assessment

Oh, Canada!

1. To answer this question, please use your globe.
   Where is the continent of North America located?

2. To answer this question, please use your map of North America.
   Where is Canada located?

3. What is the symbol of Canada?

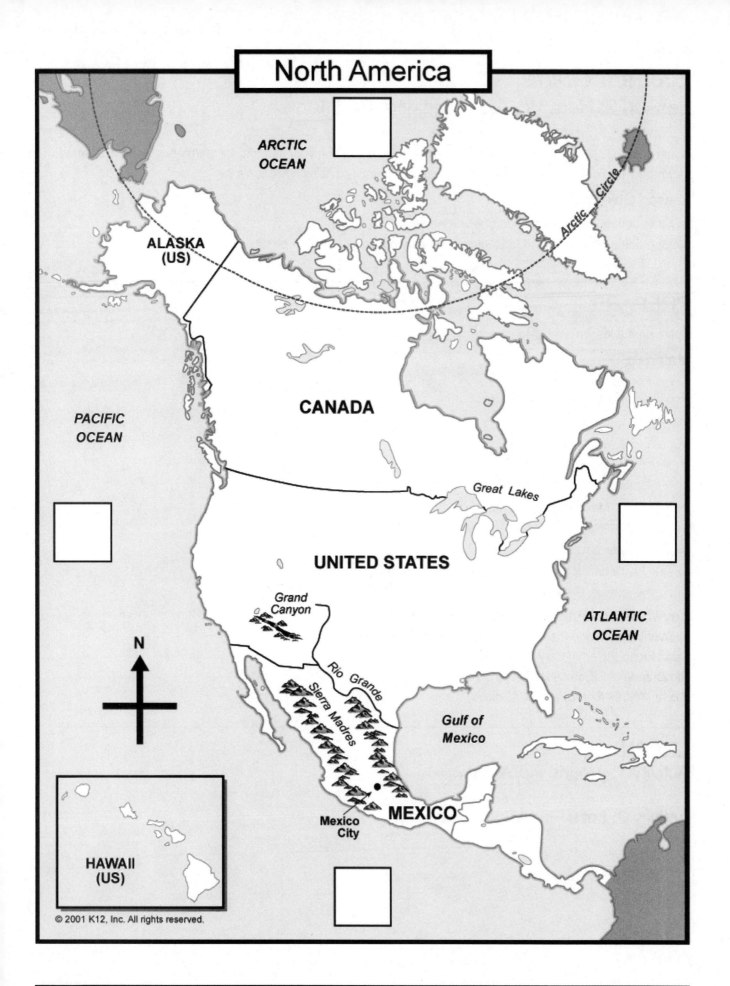

North America

ARCTIC OCEAN

ALASKA (US)

Arctic Circle

CANADA

PACIFIC OCEAN

Great Lakes

UNITED STATES

Grand Canyon

ATLANTIC OCEAN

N

Rio Grande

Sierra Madres

Gulf of Mexico

MEXICO

Mexico City

HAWAII (US)

Student Guide
Lesson 2: Here We Go to Mexico, Part 1

South of the Rio Grande lies the country of Mexico. In this lesson your student will learn about Mexico's varied geography and discover the symbolism behind the unusual picture on Mexico's flag.

Lesson Objectives

- Locate Mexico on a map of North America.
- Identify the eagle and the snake as the symbols in the center of Mexico's flag.

PREPARE

Approximate lesson time is 45 minutes.

Materials

For the Student

    Mr. Traveler Figurine

    map, world

    📖 map of North America

    crayons, 16 or more

Optional

    📖 Mexican Flag coloring sheet

    📖 Place it in Mexico activity sheet

    pencils, no. 2

    Colors of Mexico by Lynn Ainsworth Olawsky

    paper, 8 1/2" x 11"

Keywords and Pronunciation

bienvenida a Mexico (bee-en-bay-NEE-dah ah MEH-ee-ko)

hasta luego (AH-stuh loo-AY-go)

Rio Grande (REE-oh GRAHN-day)

Sierra Madres (see-ER-uh MAH-drays)

LEARN
Activity 1: Around the World *(Online)*

Activity 2: Let's Find Mexico *(Online)*

Activity 3: A Visit to Mexico *(Online)*

Activity 4. Optional: The Flag of Mexico *(Online)*

Activity 5. Optional: Place It in Mexico *(Online)*

ASSESS

Lesson Assessment: Here We Go to Mexico, Part 1 (*Online*)

You will complete an offline assessment covering the main objectives of this lesson. Your learning coach will score this assessment.

LEARN

Activity 6. Optional: Reading About the Aztec People *(Online)*

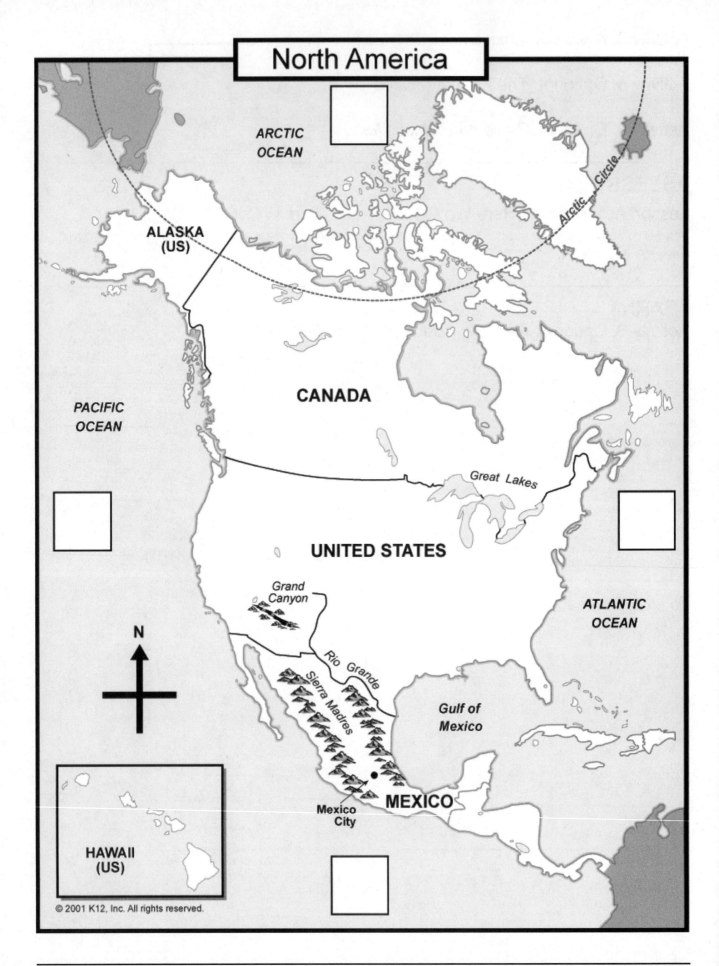

North America

ARCTIC OCEAN

ALASKA (US)

CANADA

PACIFIC OCEAN

Great Lakes

UNITED STATES

ATLANTIC OCEAN

Grand Canyon

N

Rio Grande

Sierra Madres

Gulf of Mexico

Mexico City

MEXICO

HAWAII (US)

Name _____   Date _____

Where in Mexico?

Draw a line from each term to where it can be found in Mexico.

Sierra Madre   Cactus   Sloth in the Rainforest   Rio Grande   Mexico City

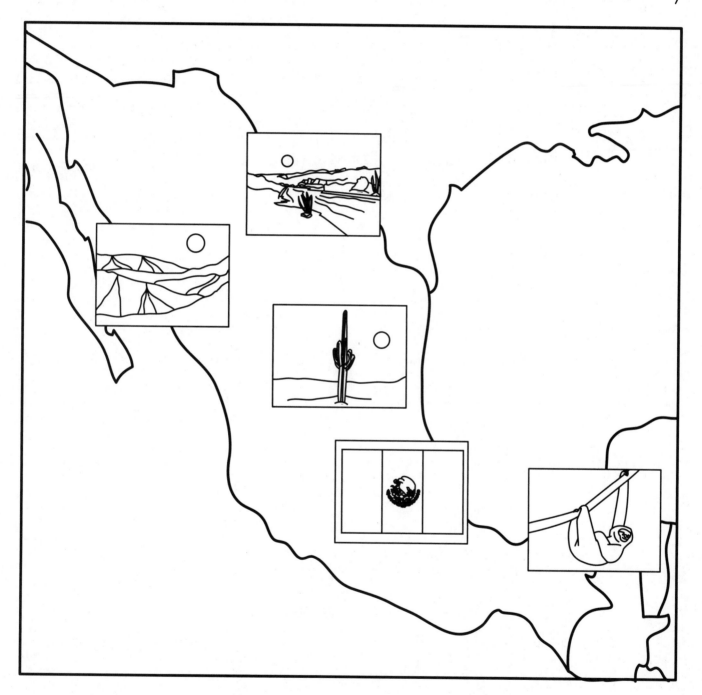

Lesson Assessment

Here We Go to Mexico, Part 1

1. To answer this question, please use your map of North America. Where is the Mexico located?

2. What two animals are shown on the Mexican flag?

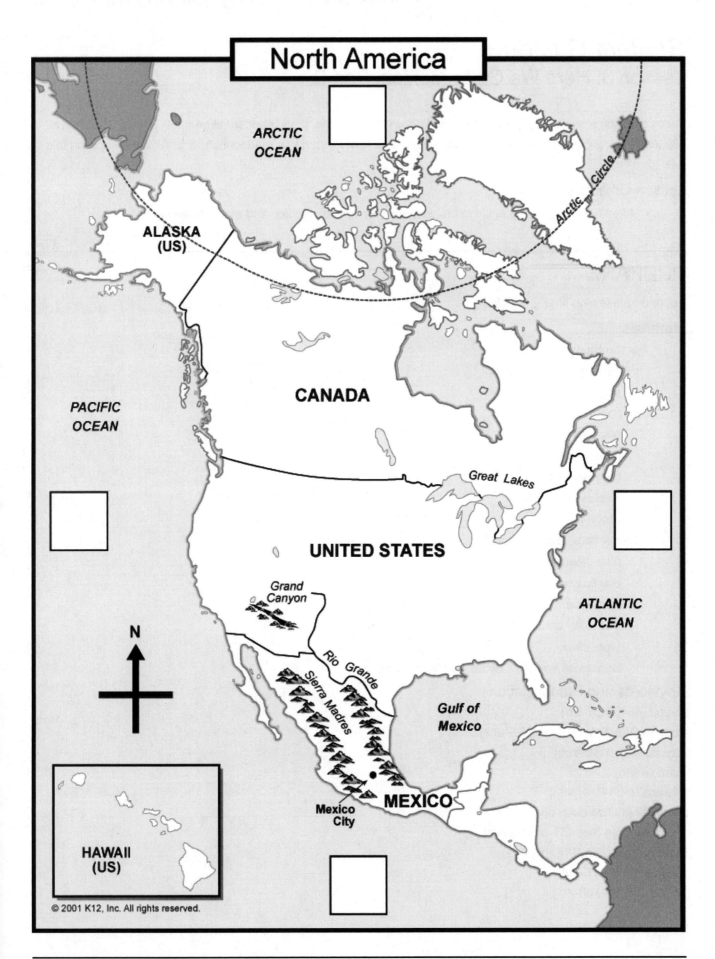

North America

ARCTIC OCEAN

ALASKA (US)

Arctic Circle

CANADA

PACIFIC OCEAN

Great Lakes

UNITED STATES

Grand Canyon

ATLANTIC OCEAN

N

Rio Grande

Sierra Madres

Gulf of Mexico

Mexico City

MEXICO

HAWAII (US)

Student Guide
Lesson 3: Here We Go to Mexico, Part 2

Today's lesson mixes many sights and sounds from Mexico--and, if you choose, even a few tastes. We'll visit a Mexican fishing village, shop in a marketplace, enjoy a fiesta, listen to a mariachi band, and read a Mexican folk tale.

Lesson Objectives

- Identify more features of life in Mexico, such as tortillas, fiestas, and mariachi music.

PREPARE

Approximate lesson time is 45 minutes.

Materials

For the Student

    🖥 map of North America

    map, world

Optional

    bag, brown paper, lunch

    beans, dried

    cups, plastic fruit

    ruler, standard 12"

    tissue paper

    markers, colored, 8 or more

    pipe cleaners

    plastic wrap

    rubber bands

    scissors, round-end safety

    tape, clear

    Borreguita and the Coyote by Verna Aardema

Keywords and Pronunciation

Ayutla (ah-YOOT-lah)

buenos dias (BWAY-nohs DEE-ahs)

cayuco (kah-YOO-koh)

Juan (wahn)

maraca (muh-RAH-kuh)

mariachi (mahr-ee-AH-chee)

Sierra Madres (see-ER-uh MAH-drays)

sombreros (suhm-BREHR-ohz)

tortillas (tawr-TEE-yuhs)

zocalo (ZHOH-koh-loh)

LEARN
Activity 1: Locate Mexico *(Online)*

Activity 2: A Day in a Fishing Village *(Online)*

Activity 3: Fiesta! *(Online)*

Activity 4: Mariachi Bands *(Online)*

Activity 5: Señor Coyote and the Sheep *(Online)*

Activity 6. Optional: Making a Maraca *(Online)*

ASSESS
Lesson Assessment: Here We Go to Mexico, Part 2 (*Online*)

You will complete an offline assessment covering the main objectives of this lesson. Your learning coach will score this assessment.

LEARN
Activity 7. Optional: The Little Lamb and the Coyote *(Online)*

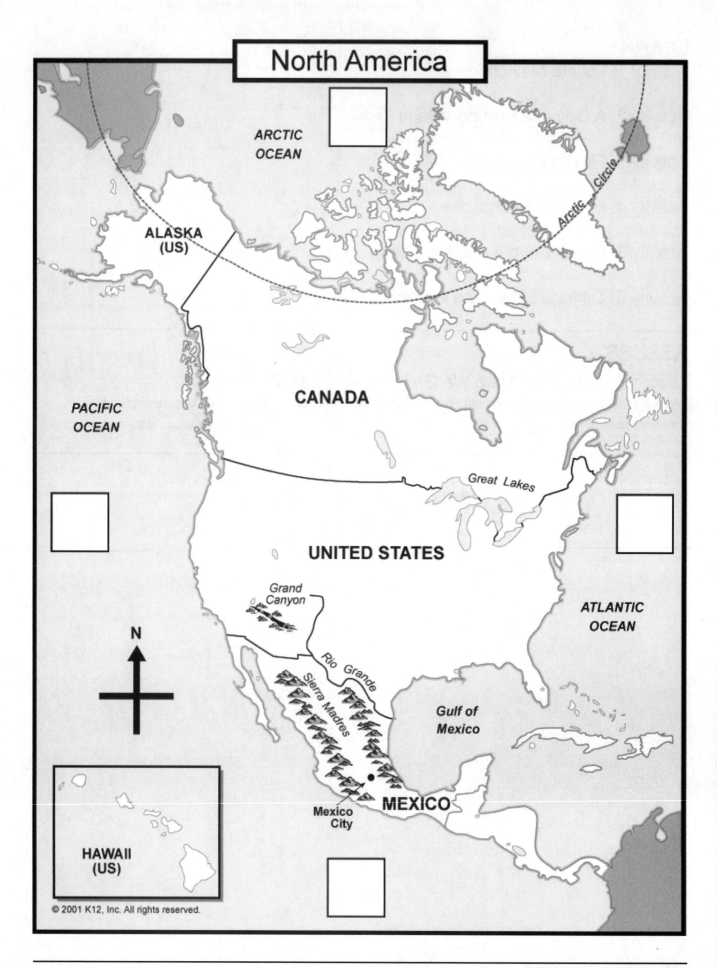

North America

ARCTIC OCEAN

ALASKA (US)

Arctic Circle

PACIFIC OCEAN

CANADA

Great Lakes

UNITED STATES

Grand Canyon

Rio Grande

Sierra Madres

ATLANTIC OCEAN

Gulf of Mexico

N

Mexico City

MEXICO

HAWAII (US)

Lesson Assessment

Here We Go to Mexico, Part 2

1. What features of life in Mexico have you have learned about?

Student Guide
Lesson 4: This Land Is Your Land

"This land is your land, this land is my land"-and this land, the United States of America, is made up of 50 states. Your student will begin the lesson by learning that 50 states make up the United States. Then he will look back at the "souvenirs" he's gathered on his trip around the world and play a game to see how much he remembers.

Lesson Objectives
- Locate the United States of America on a map of North America.
- Know that the United States of America is made up of 50 states.

PREPARE

Approximate lesson time is 45 minutes.

Materials
For the Student
- 🖳 map of North America
- crayons, 16 or more
- map, world
- stickers

Optional
- tape, masking

Keywords and Pronunciation
unite : To bring together.

LEARN
Activity 1: A Review of North America *(Online)*

Activity 2: Fifty States in the United States *(Online)*

Activity 3: Continent Review *(Online)*

ASSESS
Lesson Assessment: This Land Is Your Land (*Online*)
You will complete an offline assessment covering the main objectives of this lesson. Your learning coach will score this assessment.

LEARN
Activity 4. Optional: The Continent Twist *(Online)*

North America

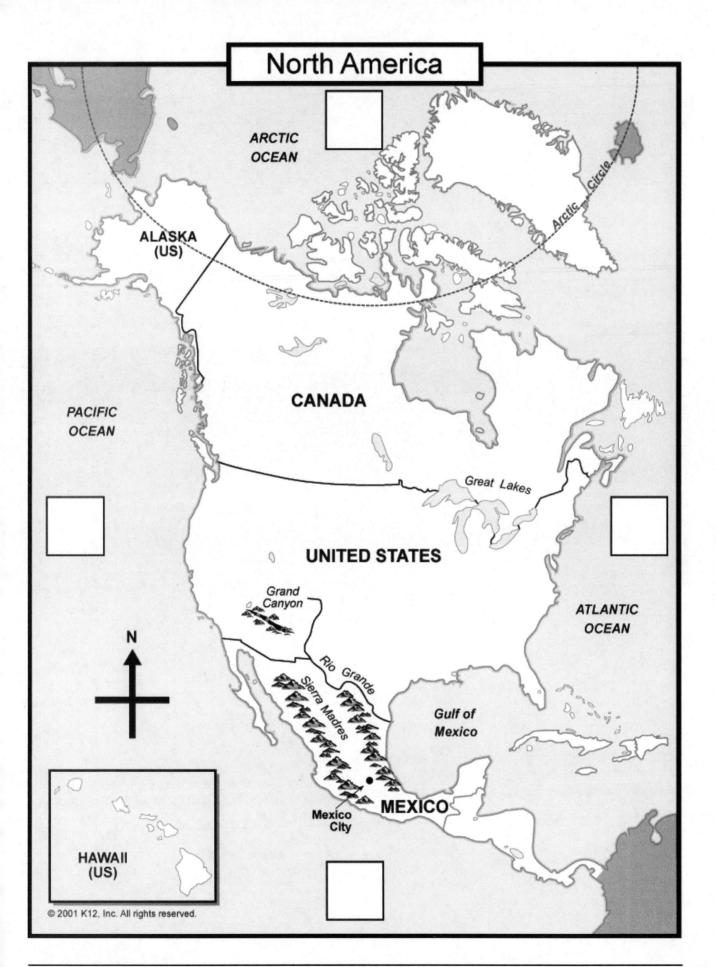

ARCTIC OCEAN

ALASKA (US)

Arctic Circle

CANADA

Great Lakes

PACIFIC OCEAN

UNITED STATES

Grand Canyon

ATLANTIC OCEAN

Rio Grande

N

Sierra Madres

Gulf of Mexico

Mexico City

MEXICO

HAWAII (US)

335

Name _____   Date _____

Lesson Assessment

This Land is Your Land

1. To answer this question, please use your map of North America. Where is the United States of America located?

2. How many states are there in all the United States?

North America

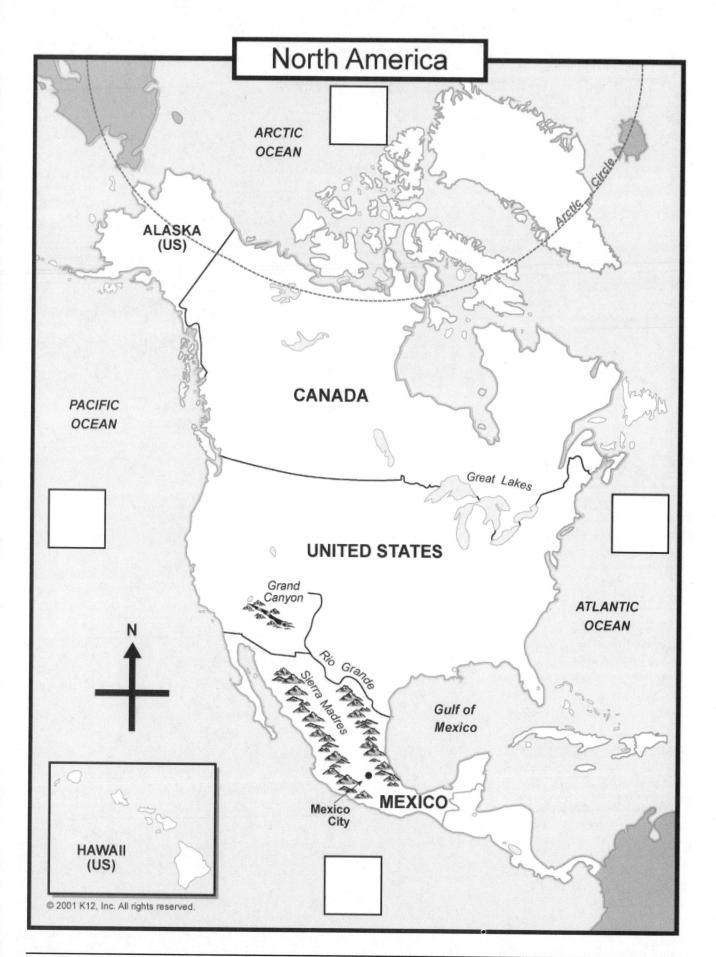

ARCTIC
OCEAN

ALASKA
(US)

Arctic Circle

CANADA

PACIFIC
OCEAN

Great Lakes

UNITED STATES

Grand
Canyon

ATLANTIC
OCEAN

N

Rio Grande

Sierra Madres

Gulf of
Mexico

Mexico
City

MEXICO

HAWAII
(US)

© 2001 K12 Inc. All rights reserved.

Student Guide
Lesson 1: From Sea to Shining Sea, Part 1

Travel from sea to shining sea to gain a closer view of the United States and its many incredible geographical features. Learn about Katharine Lee Bates, who captured the beauty of her country in song and created a work that has inspired Americans ever since.

Become familiar with major features of American geography by taking an imaginative journey with eight-year-old Katharine Lee Bates, who would grow up to write the well-known song *America the Beautiful*.

Lesson Objectives
- Identify the location of the Atlantic Ocean and the Pacific Ocean.
- Identify the location of the United States on the continent of North America.
- Locate the Appalachians, Rocky Mountains, and Mississippi River on a map of the United States.

PREPARE

Approximate lesson time is 45 minutes.

Materials
For the Student
- globe, inflatable
- map, world
- 📖 map of the United States
- 📖 America the Beautiful
- 📖 United States Map activity sheet
- paper, heavy
- crayons, 16 or more
- Elmer's Glue-All
- scissors, round-end safety

Keywords and Pronunciation
Appalachian (a-puh-LAY-chuhn)

LEARN
Activity 1: Introducing America the Beautiful *(Online)*

Activity 2: Exploring America the Beautiful *(Online)*

Activity 3: Singing America the Beautiful *(Online)*

Activity 4: Identifying Parts of America *(Online)*

Activity 5. Optional: Clap, Chant, and Color *(Online)*

ASSESS

Lesson Assessment: From Sea to Shining Sea, Part 1 (*Online*)

You will complete an offline assessment covering the main objectives of this lesson. Your learning coach will score this assessment.

LEARN

Activity 6. Optional: Traveling Across America *(Online)*

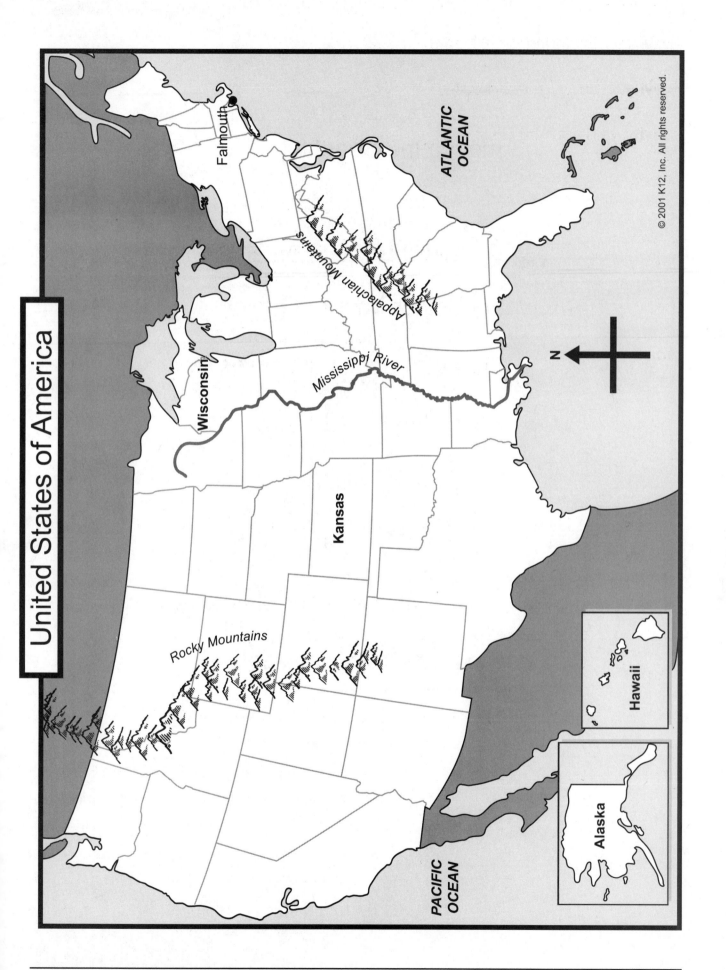

United States of America

Falmouth

ATLANTIC OCEAN

Appalachian Mountains

Mississippi River

Wisconsin

N

Kansas

Rocky Mountains

Hawaii

Alaska

PACIFIC OCEAN

America the Beautiful

O beautiful for spacious skies,

For amber waves of grain,

For purple mountain majesties

Above the fruited plain.

America! America!

God shed his grace on thee

And crown thy good with brotherhood

From sea to shining sea!

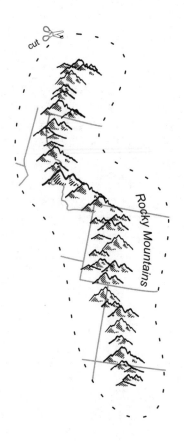

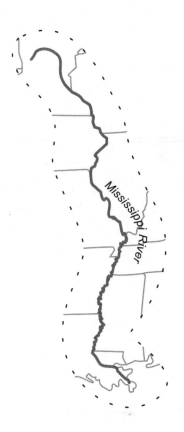

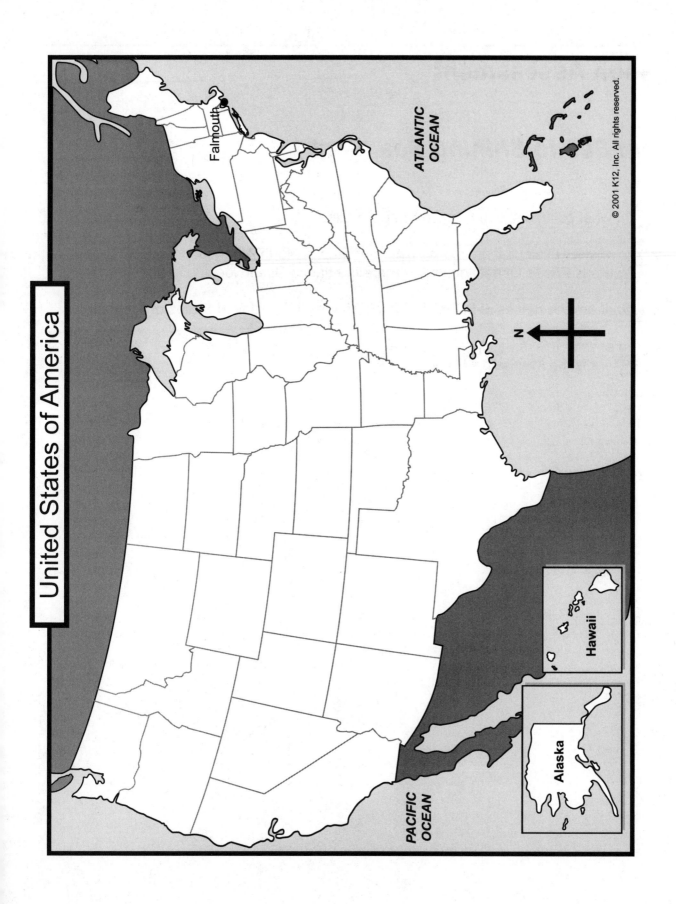

United States of America

Falmouth

ATLANTIC OCEAN

N

Hawaii

Alaska

PACIFIC OCEAN

Lesson Assessment

From Sea to Shining Sea, Part 1

1. On what continent is the United States located?

2. To answer this question, please use your map of North America.
   Where is Pacific Ocean located? Where is Atlantic Ocean located?

3. What are the names of the big mountain ranges in the United States of America?

4. To answer this question, please use your map of North America.
   Where is the Mississippi River located?

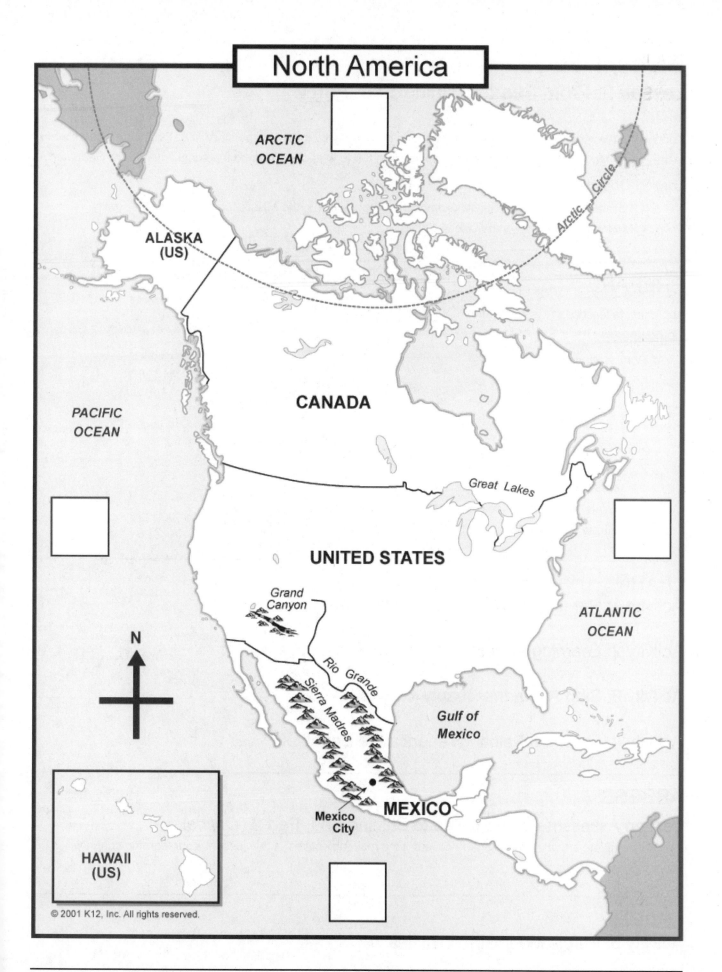

North America

ARCTIC
OCEAN

ALASKA
(US)

Arctic Circle

CANADA

PACIFIC
OCEAN

Great Lakes

UNITED STATES

N

Grand
Canyon

Rio Grande

Sierra Madres

ATLANTIC
OCEAN

Gulf of
Mexico

Mexico
City

MEXICO

HAWAII
(US)

Student Guide
Lesson 2: From Sea to Shining Sea, Part 2

Continue to learn more major features of American geography by following the story of Katharine Lee Bates's trip to the Rocky Mountains. Find out how this trip inspired her to write the words to the song *America the Beautiful*.

Lesson Objectives

- Locate the Atlantic and Pacific Oceans, the Appalachians, the Mississippi River, and the Rocky Mountains on a map of the United States.

PREPARE

Approximate lesson time is 45 minutes.

Materials

For the Student

   📖 map of the United States

   map, world

   📖 Words to America the Beautiful

Optional

   paper, heavy

   brush, watercolor

   paints, watercolor, 8 colors or more

   Purple Mountain Majesties by Barbara Younger

LEARN
Activity 1: Remembering Katharine Lee Bates *(Online)*

Activity 2: Learning About the Beauty of America *(Online)*

Activity 3: Sing About the Beauty *(Online)*

Activity 4. Optional: Painting America the Beautiful *(Online)*

ASSESS

Lesson Assessment: From Sea to Shining Sea, Part 2 *(Online)*

You will complete an offline assessment covering the main objectives of this lesson. Your learning coach will score this assessment.

LEARN
Activity 5: Purple Mountain Majesties *(Online)*

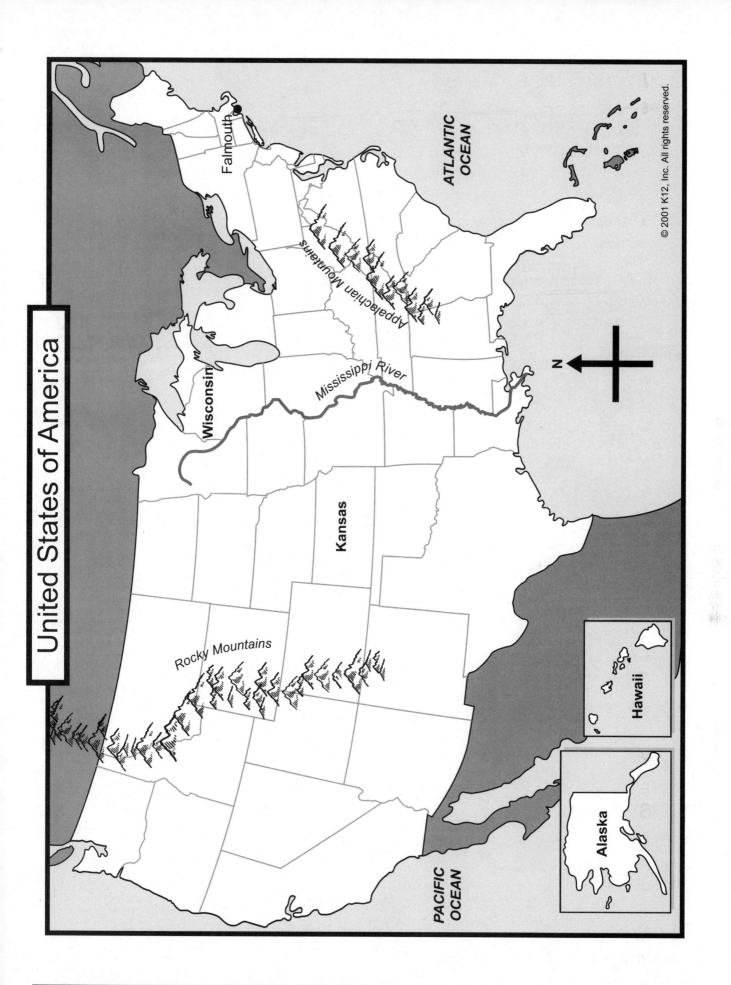

United States of America

Falmouth

ATLANTIC OCEAN

Appalachian Mountains

Wisconsin

Mississippi River

N

Kansas

Rocky Mountains

PACIFIC OCEAN

Hawaii

Alaska

America the Beautiful

O beautiful for spacious skies,

For amber waves of grain,

For purple mountain majesties

Above the fruited plain.

America! America!

God shed his grace on thee

And crown thy good with brotherhood

From sea to shining sea!

Lesson Assessment

From Sea to Shining Sea, Part 2

1. To answer this question, please use your map of North America. Where is the Atlantic Ocean located?

2. To answer this question, please use your map of North America. Where is the Pacific Ocean located?

3. To answer this question, please use your map of North America. Where is the Mississippi River located?

4. To answer this question, please use your map of North America. Where are the Rocky Mountains located?

5. To answer this question, please use your map of North America. Where are the Appalachian Mountains located?

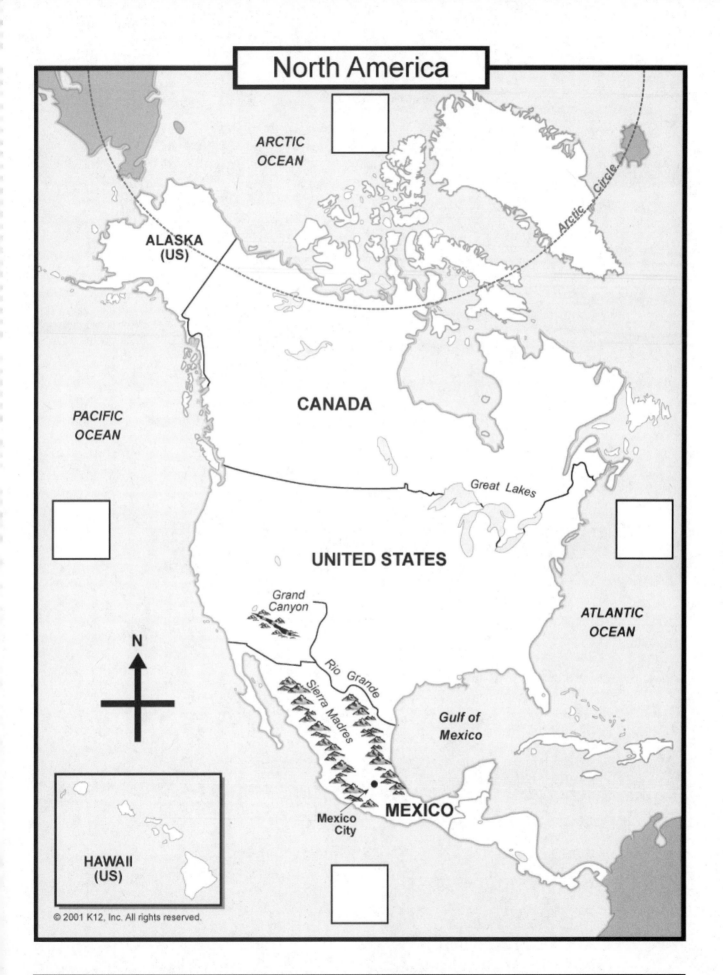

North America

ARCTIC OCEAN

ALASKA (US)

Arctic Circle

CANADA

PACIFIC OCEAN

Great Lakes

UNITED STATES

Grand Canyon

ATLANTIC OCEAN

N

Rio Grande

Sierra Madres

Gulf of Mexico

Mexico City

MEXICO

HAWAII (US)

Student Guide
Lesson 1: The Ancestral Pueblo of the Southwest

Journey far back in time to meet the peoples who were the "first Americans." Visit the Ancestral Pueblo of the southwest, the Indians of the Great Plains, and the Eastern Woodland tribes. Learn where these Indians lived and how they met their needs for food, clothing, and shelter.

Lesson Objectives

- Locate where the Anasazi once lived.
- Identify the Anasazi as an American Indian tribe who once inhabited the American Southwest.
- Tell that the Anasazi lived in villages called pueblos.

PREPARE

Approximate lesson time is 45 minutes.

Materials

For the Student

   🖳 map of the First Americans

   crayons, 16 or more

   When Clay Sings by Byrd Baylor (ISBN 0689711069)

Optional

   🖳 Paint Your Pot activity sheet

   paintbrush

   paints, watercolor, 8 colors or more

   glue sticks

   paper, colored construction, 12"x12"

Keywords and Pronunciation

adobe (uh-DOH-bee)

Anasazi (ah-nuh-SAH-zee)

Apache (uh-PA-chee)

Hopi (HOH-pee)

Navajo (NAH-vuh-hoh)

pueblo (PWEH-bloh)

Zuni (ZOO-nee)

LEARN
Activity 1: Reviewing America the Beautiful *(Online)*

Activity 2: Native Americans *(Online)*

Activity 3: Life for the Ancestral Pueblo *(Online)*

Activity 4: Read Aloud *(Online)*

Activity 5. Optional: Paint Your Pot *(Offline)*

ASSESS
Lesson Assessment: The Ancestral Pueblo of the Southwest (*Online*)

You will complete an offline assessment covering the main objectives of this lesson. Your learning coach will score this assessment.

LEARN
Activity 6. Optional: Pot Puzzle *(Online)*

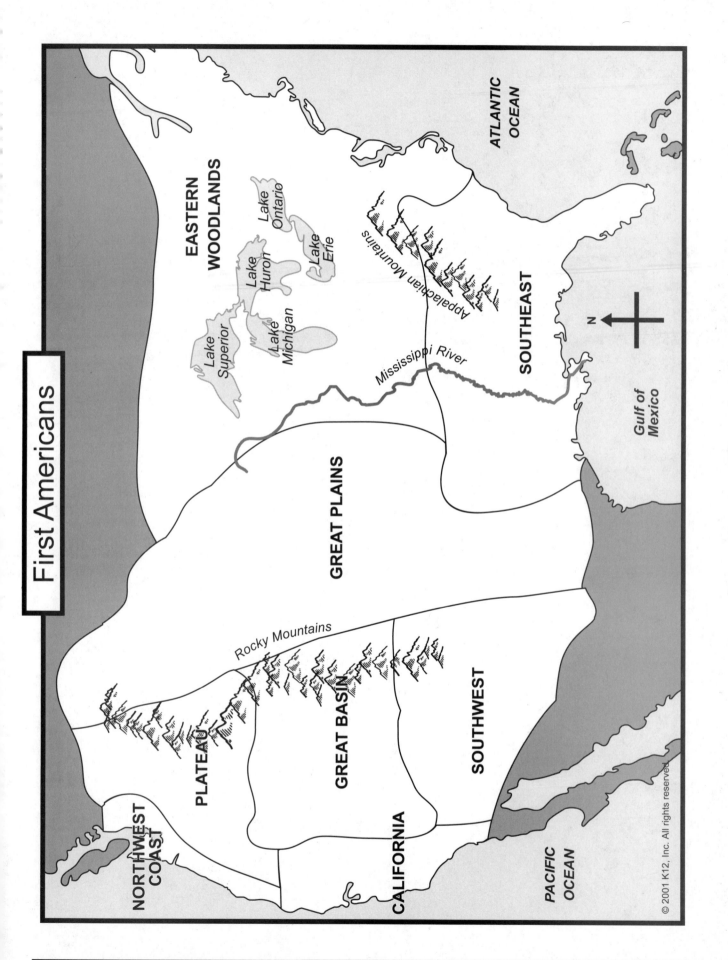

First Americans

EASTERN WOODLANDS

Lake Superior
Lake Michigan
Lake Huron
Lake Erie
Lake Ontario

ATLANTIC OCEAN

Appalachian Mountains

Mississippi River

SOUTHEAST

Gulf of Mexico

N

GREAT PLAINS

Rocky Mountains

PLATEAU

GREAT BASIN

SOUTHWEST

NORTHWEST COAST

CALIFORNIA

PACIFIC OCEAN

Paint Your Pot

Lesson Assessment

The Ancestral Pueblo of the Southwest

1. Name the American-Indian tribe who once inhabited the American Southwest.

2. What was an Anasazi, (Ancestral Pueblo), village called?

3. To answer this question, please use the map of the First Americans. Locate on the map where the Anasazi, (Ancestral Pueblo), once lived.

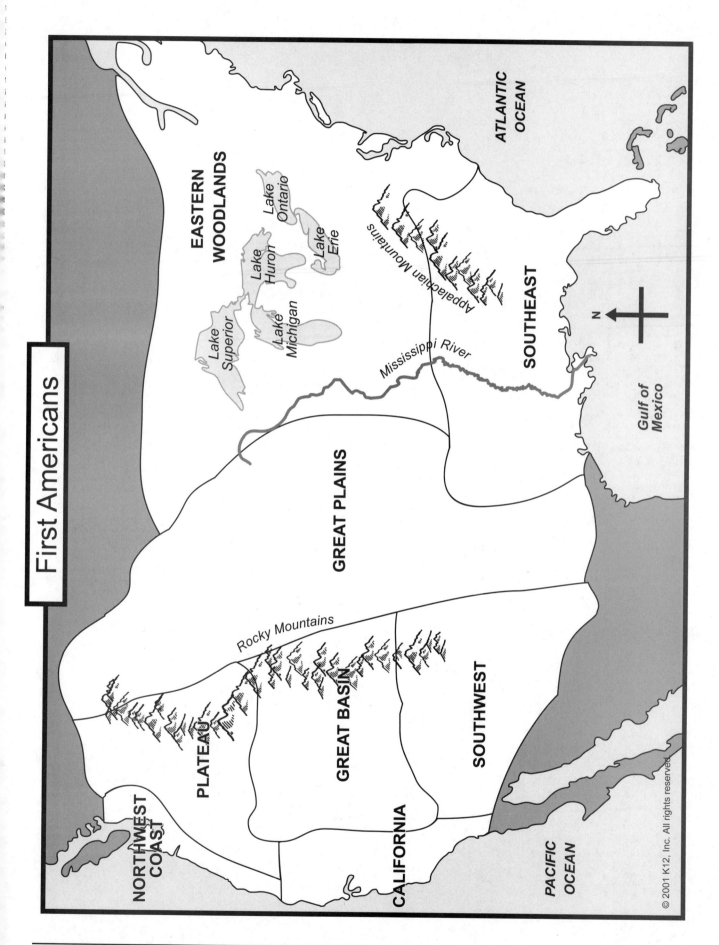

First Americans

EASTERN WOODLANDS

ATLANTIC OCEAN

Lake Ontario
Lake Erie
Lake Huron
Lake Superior
Lake Michigan

Appalachian Mountains

Mississippi River

SOUTHEAST

Gulf of Mexico

N

GREAT PLAINS

Rocky Mountains

PLATEAU

GREAT BASIN

SOUTHWEST

NORTHWEST COAST

CALIFORNIA

PACIFIC OCEAN

Paint Your Pot

Student Guide
Lesson 2: The Plains Indians

The Plains Indians lived between the Mississippi River and the Rocky Mountains. Some tribes farmed, while others followed and hunted the buffalo.

Lesson Objectives

- Locate the Great Plains on a map.
- Identify the Plains Indians as hunters of buffalo.

PREPARE

Approximate lesson time is 45 minutes.

Materials

For the Student

    📖 map of the First Americans

    crayons, 16 or more

Optional

    bags, brown paper grocery

    twig

    scissors, round-end safety

    string

    tape, clear

    The Gift of the Sacred Dog by Paul Goble

Keywords and Pronunciation

Cheyenne (shiy-AN)

Comanche (kuh-MAN-chee)

tipis (TEE-pees)

LEARN
Activity 1: Reviewing Anasazi *(Online)*

Activity 2: The American Indians of the Great Plains *(Online)*

Activity 3: How the Buffalo Came to the People *(Online)*

Activity 4. Optional: Making a Tipi *(Online)*

ASSESS

Lesson Assessment: The Plains Indians (*Online*)

You will complete an offline assessment covering the main objectives of this lesson. Your learning coach will score this assessment.

LEARN

Activity 5. Optional: Read The Gift of the Sacred Dog *(Online)*

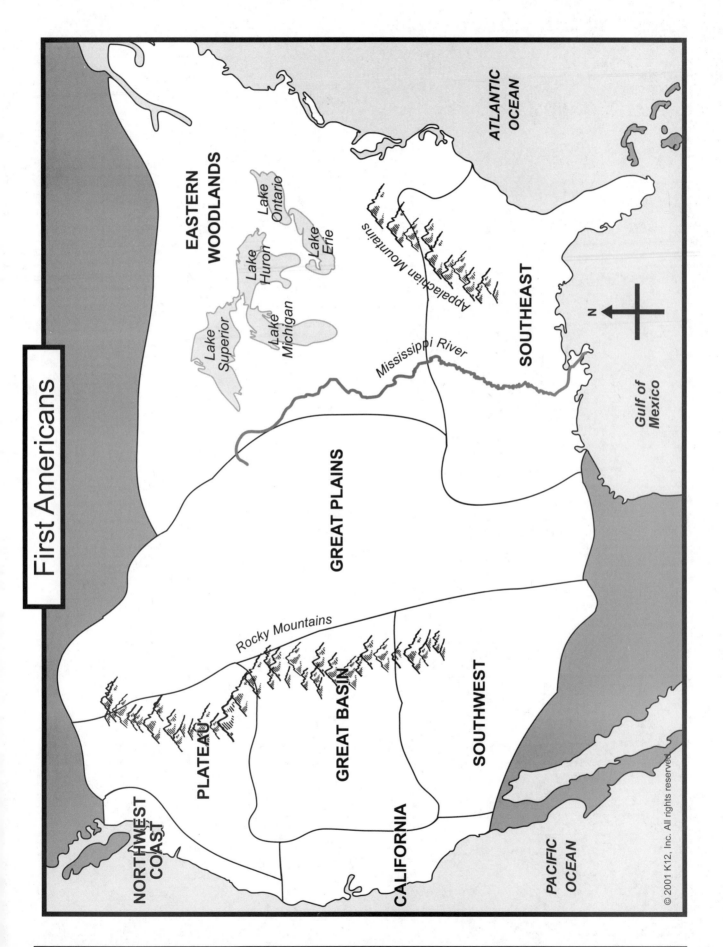

First Americans

EASTERN WOODLANDS

Lake Superior
Lake Michigan
Lake Huron
Lake Erie
Lake Ontario

ATLANTIC OCEAN

Appalachian Mountains

SOUTHEAST

Mississippi River

Gulf of Mexico

N

GREAT PLAINS

Rocky Mountains

PLATEAU

GREAT BASIN

SOUTHWEST

NORTHWEST COAST

CALIFORNIA

PACIFIC OCEAN

Lesson Assessment

The Plains Indians

1. To answer this question, please use the map of the First Americans. Color the Great Plains on the map.

2. What animal did the Plains Indian hunt?

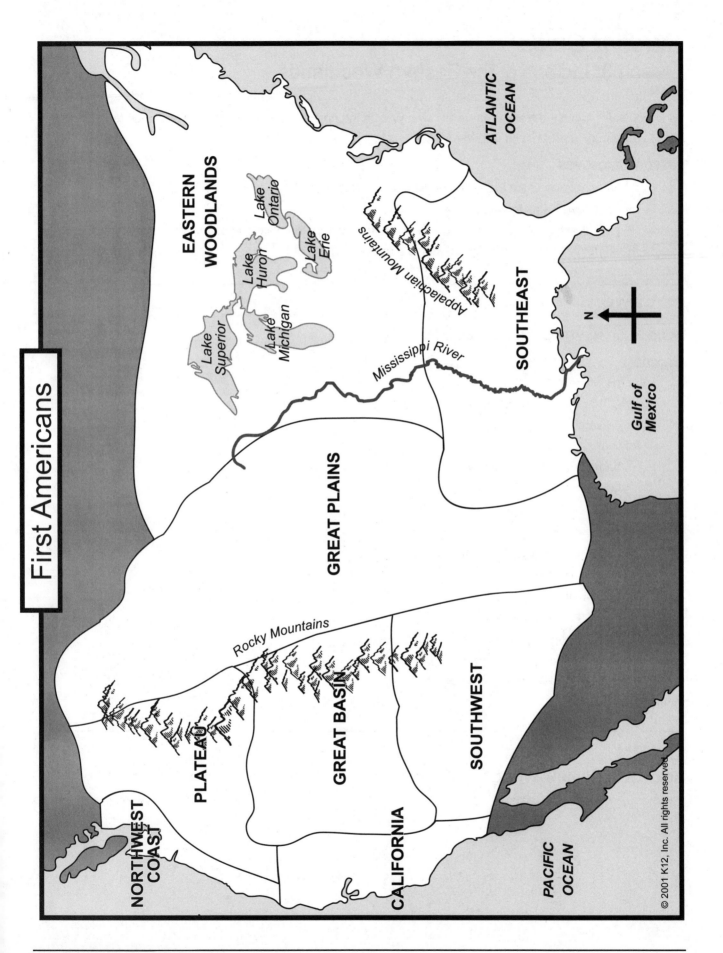

First Americans

EASTERN WOODLANDS

ATLANTIC OCEAN

Lake Ontario

Lake Erie

Lake Huron

Lake Michigan

Lake Superior

Appalachian Mountains

SOUTHEAST

Mississippi River

Gulf of Mexico

N

GREAT PLAINS

Rocky Mountains

PLATEAU

GREAT BASIN

SOUTHWEST

NORTHWEST COAST

CALIFORNIA

PACIFIC OCEAN

Student Guide
Lesson 3: Indians of the Eastern Woodlands

Today we learn about the Native Americans who lived in the northeast, in the Eastern Woodlands region. We meet two Abenaki children, and we hear an Iroquois legend.

Lesson Objectives

- Locate the area of the Eastern Woodlands on a map.
- Name wigwams as the homes that the Abenaki built.
- Explain that the Abenaki relied on and made good use of the plant and animal resources in the Eastern Woodlands for their food, homes, clothing, and more.

PREPARE

Approximate lesson time is 45 minutes.

Materials

For the Student

    🖳 map of First Americans

    crayons, 16 or more

Optional

    bags, brown paper grocery

    glue sticks

    twig

    string

    paper, colored construction, 12"x12"

    Elmer's Glue-All

    pipe cleaners (6)

    scissors, round-end safety

Keywords and Pronunciation

Abenaki (ah-bih-NAH-kee)

Haudenosaunee (hoh-dee-noh-SHOH-nee)

Iroquois (IR-uh-kwoy)

LEARN
Activity 1: Review What You Know *(Online)*

Activity 2: The Eastern Woodlands *(Online)*

Activity 3: Little Thunder and Running Brook Help the Family *(Online)*

Activity 4: Read Aloud: Catching a Porcupine *(Online)*

Activity 5: How Chipmunk Got His Stripes *(Online)*

Activity 6. Optional: Make a Wigwam *(Online)*

ASSESS
Lesson Assessment: Indians of the Eastern Woodlands (*Online*)
You will complete an offline assessment covering the main objectives of this lesson. Your learning coach will score this assessment.

LEARN
Activity 7: The People of the Longhouse *(Online)*

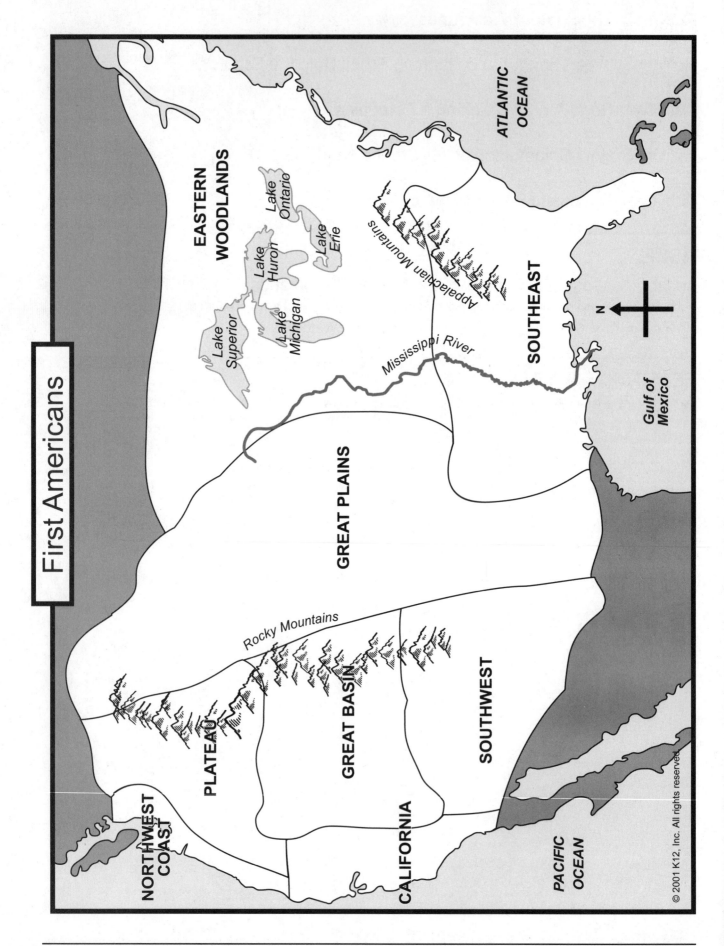

First Americans

EASTERN WOODLANDS

Lake Ontario
Lake Erie
Lake Huron
Lake Michigan
Lake Superior

Appalachian Mountains

Mississippi River

SOUTHEAST

ATLANTIC OCEAN

Gulf of Mexico

N

GREAT PLAINS

Rocky Mountains

PLATEAU

GREAT BASIN

SOUTHWEST

NORTHWEST COAST

CALIFORNIA

PACIFIC OCEAN

Lesson Assessment

Indians of the Eastern Woodlands

1. To answer this question, please use the map of the First Americans. Where are the the Eastern Woodlands?

2. What was the name of the homes the Abenaki built from bark?

3. Where did the Abenaki people find what they needed to live?

4. What are some examples of the food and clothing the Abenaki made from the plants and animals in the Eastern Woodlands?

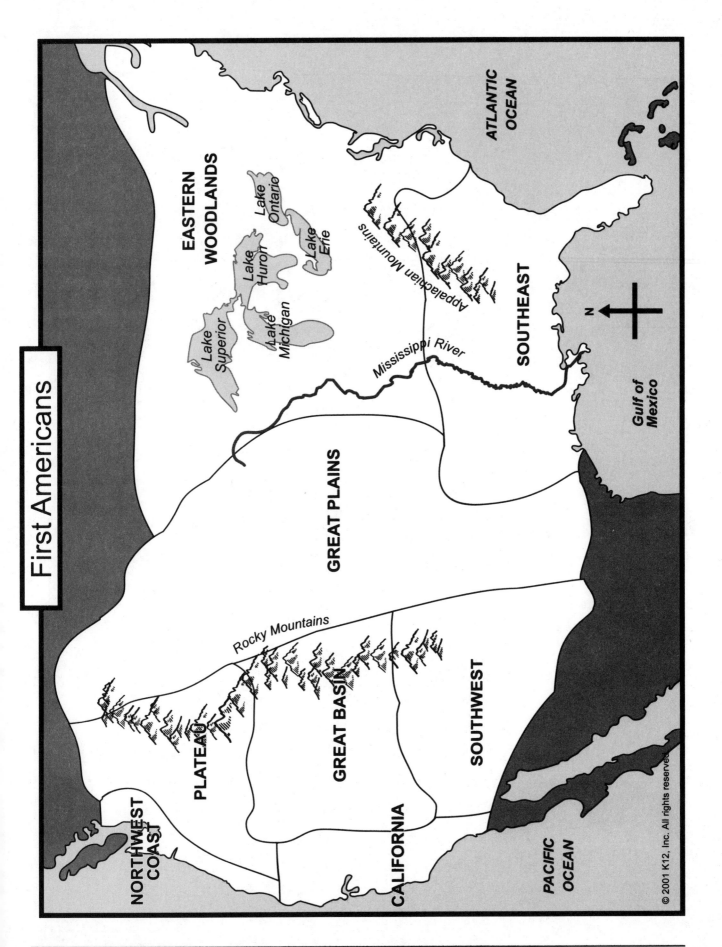

First Americans

EASTERN WOODLANDS

Lake Ontario
Lake Erie
Lake Huron
Lake Michigan
Lake Superior

ATLANTIC OCEAN

Appalachian Mountains

SOUTHEAST

Mississippi River

Gulf of Mexico

N

GREAT PLAINS

Rocky Mountains

PLATEAU

GREAT BASIN

SOUTHWEST

NORTHWEST COAST

CALIFORNIA

PACIFIC OCEAN

Answer Keys

Lesson Assessment Answer Key

Our Home, Our Earth

Answers:

1. Earth
2. Earth
3. Seven

Lesson Assessment Answer Key

Name That Continent

1. map of the world or world map
2. Your student should name the continents and the sight associated with it correctly.

Lesson Assessment Answer Key

Moving in the Right Direction

Answers:

1. You student should move Mr. Traveler north, south, east, and west.

2. Mr. Traveler is moved to the North and South Poles.

Lesson Assessment Answer Key

Get Ready to Travel

1. Answers may vary, but North America most common response.
2. Answers may vary, but most common response should be United States of America.
3. Move Mr. Traveler in a circle around the continent on which you live and around the country in which you live.

Lesson Assessment Answer Key

Animals of the Outback

Answers.

1. Australia is located Southeast of Asia.

2. Answers should include three of the following:
   echidna
   emu
   platypus
   kangaroo
   koala

3. a continent

Name _____   Date _____

Lesson Assessment Answer Key

Outback and City

Answers

1. Your student should point to the coastline of Australia.

2. Yes.

Lesson Assessment Answer Key

Let's Visit Spain

Answers.

1. Europe is North of Africa.

2. A country is part of a continent.

3. Europe

Name _____ Date _____

Lesson Assessment Answer Key

Let's Visit England

Answers.

1. Europe is north of Africa.

2. Europe

3. It is an island because it is a piece of land surrounded by water.

Lesson Assessment Answer Key

Let's Visit France

1. Europe

2. Answers should include two of the following:
   Eiffel Tower
   Cathedral of Notre Dame
   Sacré-Coeur
   the Louvre

Lesson Assessment Answer Key

Let's Visit Ireland

Answers.

1. Ireland is located off the west coast of Great Britain.

2. Answers should include two of the following:
    leprechauns
    shamrocks
    green
    island
    Emerald Isle

3. It's a small island that is very green.

Lesson Assessment Answer Key

Germany and Brothers Grimm

Answers.

1. Europe is north of Africa.

2. Europe

3. borders

4. The Brothers Grimm collected many fairy tales, such as Snow White.

Lesson Assessment Answer Key

Let's Visit Italy and Wave Good-bye to Europe

Answers.

1. Spain is on the far western side of Europe, just above Africa.

2. East.

3. Europe

Lesson Assessment Answer Key

Slow Boat Through China

1. Asia is east of Europe.

2. Russia is the northernmost country in Asia.

3. China is south of Russia and northeast of India.

4. Yes

Lesson Assessment Answer Key

A Tour of Japan

1. Asia

2. Islands

3. Japan

Lesson Assessment Answer Key

Into India

Answers.

1. India contains the city New Delhi.

2. Asia

3. a river

4. The Himalaya Mountains stretch across the northern border of India.

Lesson Assessment Answer Key

The Arabian Peninsula

Answers

1. Saudia Arabia contains the city Riyadh.

2. Answers may vary but should contain information about the Roc are very large birds, Sindbad gets gems and escapes by placing meat on his back and having a Roc carry him away.

3. a peninsula

Lesson Assessment Answer Key

Life in the Sahara

Answers.

1. Africa is south of Europe.

2. the Sahara Desert

3. Africa

4. A desert is a dry area, usually covered with sand.

Lesson Assessment Answer Key

The African Savanna

Answers.

1. grassland

2. lions, zebras, giraffes

Name _____   Date _____

Lesson Assessment Answer Key

Central Africa and the Congo Rain Forest

Answers.

1. The Sahara is a part of northern Africa.

2. The savanna is a part of central and eastern Africa.

3. The Congo River flows from south-central Africa north and west past Kinshasa.

4. Answers may vary but could include: it's near the equator; it's warm and sticky; a lot of animals live in it; it rains a lot; it's hot

Lesson Assessment Answer Key

African Villages and Cities

1. The Sahara is a part of northern Africa. The savanna is a part of central and eastern Africa. The rain forest is a part of west-central Africa.

2. in villages and cities

Lesson Assessment Answer Key

The Amazon Rain Forest

Answers.

1. South America is located south of North America.

2. The Amazon River and the Amazon rain forest are located in the north-central part of South America.

3. In the different layers.

Lesson Assessment Answer Key

It Comes From Brazil

1. Brazil is on the far east portion of South America. It contains the city of Rio de Janeiro.

2. Answers may vary but should include two of the following: coffee, sugar, oranges, and rubber.

Lesson Assessment Answer Key

High in the Andes

Answers.

1. The Andes Mountains are along the western edge of South America.

2. Answers may vary but may include people live very high in the mountains, there is no electricity, people dig terraces or steps into the hillside to plant, animals sleep inside to stay warm, they haul water for washing and cooking.

Lesson Assessment Answer Key

On the Pampas

Answers.

1. The pampas are in southern South America to the east of the Andes Mountains.

2. pampas

3. a South American cowboy

Lesson Assessment Answer Key

Land of Ice and Snow

Answers.

1. Antarctica is located on the bottom of the globe.

2. The South Pole is just southwest of the center of Antarctica.

3. no

Lesson Assessment Answer Key

Penguins in Antarctica

Answers.

1. yes

2. yes

3. Antarctica is located on the bottom of the globe.

4. Antarctica

Name _____   Date _____

Lesson Assessment Answer Key

Oh, Canada!

Answers.

1. North America is north of South America. It consist of Canada, the United States of America, and Mexico.

2. Canada is north of the United States.

3. Maple Leaf

Lesson Assessment Answer Key

Here We Go to Mexico, Part 1

Answers.

1. Mexico is just south of the United States.

2. an eagle and a snake

Lesson Assessment Answer Key

Here We Go to Mexico, Part 2

Answers.

1. Answers vary but should include tortillas, fiestas, and mariachi music.

Lesson Assessment Answer Key

This Land is Your Land

Answers.

1. The United States of America is just north of Mexico.

2. Fifty

Lesson Assessment Answer Key

From Sea to Shining Sea, Part 1

Answers.

1. North America

2. The Pacific Ocean is on the west of the United States of America and the Atlantic is on the east.

3. The Appalachian Mountains and the Rocky Mountains.

4. The Mississippi River is near the center of the United States of America.

Lesson Assessment Answer Key

From Sea to Shining Sea, Part 2

Answers.

1. The Atlantic Ocean is on the east of the United States of America.

2. The Pacific Ocean is on the west of the United States of America.

3. The Mississippi River is in the center of the United States of America.

4. The Rocky Mountains are on the western side of the United States of America.

5. The Appalachian Mountains are on the eastern side of the United States of America.

Lesson Assessment Answer Key

The Ancestral Pueblo of the Southwest

Answers.

1. the Anasazi, (Ancestral Pueblo)

2. a pueblo

3. The Anasazi, (Ancestral Pueblo), lived in the Southwest region of the United States.

Lesson Assessment Answer Key

The Plains Indians

Answers.

1. The Great Plains are in the center of the United States.

2. buffalo

Name _____   Date _____

Lesson Assessment Answer Key

Indians of the Eastern Woodlands

Answers.

1. The the Eastern Woodlands are in the Eastern region of the United States.

2. the wigwam

3. They made good use of the plant and animal resources in the Eastern Woodlands.

4. Answers will vary, but may include clothing such as moccasins, decorations such as porcupine quills, and food such as bear, moose and deer.